In These Veins

*Stories of Life on
a Small American Farm*

Doug Glorie

In These Veins: Stories of Life on a Small American Farm
Copyright © 2024 Doug Glorie

Produced and printed by Stillwater River Publications.
All rights reserved. Written and produced in the United States of America.
This book may not be reproduced or sold in any form without the expressed, written permission of the author(s) and publisher.

Visit our website at
www.StillwaterPress.com
for more information.

First Stillwater River Publications Edition

ISBN: 978-1-963296-61-7

1 2 3 4 5 6 7 8 9 10

Names: Glorie, Doug, author.
Title: In these veins : stories of life on a small American farm / Doug Glorie.
Description: First Stillwater River Publications edition. | West Warwick, RI, USA : Stillwater River Publications, [2024]
Identifiers: ISBN: 978-1-963296-61-7
Subjects: LCSH: Glorie, Doug. | Farmers—New York (State)—Biography. | Farm life—New York (State) | Gardening. | Nature. | LCGFT: Autobiographies. | Essays.
Classification: LCC: S417.G56 I5 2024 | DDC: 630.92—dc23

Written by Doug Glorie.
Edited by MaryEllen Glorie.
Cover and interior design by Elisha Gillette.
Published by Stillwater River Publications,
West Warwick, RI, USA.

The views and opinions expressed in this book are solely those of the author(s) and do not necessarily reflect the views and opinions of the publisher.

IN THESE VEINS

Table of Contents

Prologue 1
Aardvark 5
Frenchie and the Doodlebug 11
Rabbit Trap 15
The Art of Sledding 19
Potato Days 25
The '53 Chevrolet 45
The Family Garden 49
Black Tuesday 53
Pay Me One Dollar 59
Firewood 65
Another Broken Rib 71
Stone Walls 75
Barn on Fire 79
French Drains 81
The Massey Ferguson 85
Farm Dog 91
It's Spring—Let's Move the Pigs 97
The Gasket 101
Scorched Orchard 105
Wildlife, Livestock, and "He Just Served Her" 109
The Cows Are Out Again 115
Row Not Straight 123
Ten Thousand Trees 127
Stand Back from The Window 131
Belted Bartletts 139
Please Buy My Ida Reds 143

Steer Into the Skid. 149
Day Trading 155
Negotiation. 159
The List 165
The Farm Wife. 169
Who Shot the Deer?. 173
A New Apple. 177
Iowa Chief 181
Railroad in the Woods. 187
Living With Wildlife 191
Don't Look Away. 199
Diversification 205
Gravity is Your Friend. 213
Birth of a Winery 219
A Coalition. 235
Live Until Tomorrow 239
Physics and Farming. 245
Found It!. 253
How Does a Farmer Retire?. 265
Paradise. 269
D3. 275
Seeking Success 279
Save The Ridge. 285
Savor Simple 289
Epilogue 293

Ten Reasons to Become a Farmer 296
Farm Glossary 297
Noteworthy Sayings 302
Acknowledgements 304
About the Author 306

Prologue

I WROTE *In These Veins* BECAUSE I FELT THAT MANY OF THE experiences that I enjoyed or endured or found comical during the past seventy-six years were worth putting into print. You will read more than fifty stories grounded in farming (pun intended) that I want to share with you, all of which can stand on their own, but they are sequenced in an order that I feel makes the most sense. The book was conceptually planned to be a memoir but gradually morphed into much more. As I moved memories from my brain to print, I realized that the reader could enjoy a better reading experience if I shared why I chose to execute a strategy a certain way, including the thought processes involved. I also introduced how the sciences of biology, physics, chemistry, and meteorology play major roles in the success or failure of a farm in any one calendar year.

Much has changed during my seven-plus decades, and I believe it is important to jot down a few notes to that effect. Otherwise, how will future generations know that doctors once made house calls, that phones had cords and slow-moving rotary dials, were available only in black, and a person at the other end after dialing "0" was called an "Operator," that cows were milked by pulling on their teats, engineers solved complex mathematical equations with a slide rule, gasoline was eighteen cents per gallon, and the attendant washed your car or truck windshield while they filled up your tank.

Nearly all my stories depict an agricultural lifestyle full of unique challenges, inspiring successes, unpredictable adventures, and the occasional failure. Farming is unlike any other occupation, where the mother—not the father—controls the annual financial outcome in any one calendar year. I am referring to Mother Nature, where a ten-minute hailstorm in August or a twenty-six-degree frost in May can instantly turn what would have been a sizable profit into a partial or even total loss. Once we've finished spewing the usual curse words after such a distressing incident, there is really nothing to do but slowly shake our heads, think to ourselves, *There is always next year*, and soldier on.

I think the "next year" thing is worth fleshing out. Last fall, I was driving on one of our town roads when I noticed a used landscape rake for sale on the edge of the road; a ripped piece of brown cardboard with a phone number scrawled on it was propped against the rake. I didn't recognize the number, but I called it. The man who answered identified himself as Joe, and I realized by the sound of his voice that I knew him. He and I agreed to meet a couple hours later. The rake's original yellow factory paint was all but a memory; there were four tines missing, and five were broken. We dickered a bit about the price, and I wrote out a check. We shared a couple of quick stories about the price of apples, the out-of-control deer population, and the pending election. As we wrapped up our conversation and I prepared to depart, Joe said to me, "Doug, you know that this coming spring will be my forty-third season growing apples, and I am excited."

He said it with a smile and a watery eye, and that is exactly how I embrace each new year as well!

ONE

Aardvark

*The trials and tribulations
of owning farm equipment.*

OUR TENURE ON THE FARM BEGAN WITH RAISING BEEF CATTLE, pigs, and rabbits. It was the kind of agricultural venue that enabled me to have a job at IBM and be a farmer at the same time. At any one time, our beef on hoof inventory would range from six to fourteen head, mostly steers (castrated males) and some heifers (female non-pregnant cows), all of which were of a beef type species. We had enough pasture to carry the herd until fall but had to switch to hay and corn for the cold months. I had an arrangement with a friend of mine where I would go over to his farm every couple of weeks and get a ton of ground ear corn, also called feed corn, to feed the steers. I am frugal by nature, so I thought that I could save money by planting my own corn, harvesting it, and having it ground up. We decided to set aside a few acres to plant the feed corn. One planting was to be down along the town road, and the other one would be high on the hill.

Planting by hand as I did in the house garden was out of the question; fortunately, I was able to locate an ancient, rusty John Deere horse-drawn corn planter in a nearby town. It was already an antique, probably over fifty years old, and I guessed it hadn't been put to work in a couple of decades, but it suited my needs, and at $40, the price was right, so I purchased it. I promptly modified it so I could pull it with the three-point hitch on the back of my Massey Ferguson tractor. It wasn't elegant, but this setup worked quite well. I prepped the fields for planting, and on a warm May weekend, I seeded them with corn. Soon after, tiny plants began to emerge from the earth. The season progressed, and the plants got larger and larger. Then the thought occurred to me, how am I going to get the corn harvested? The obvious choice was to try to locate a corn picker. Carmen, a farmer friend of mine, was doing the same thing on his farm, and he was able to locate a picker just west of Ellenville, NY, about an hour's drive from me. He informed me that the farmer from whom he had bought his picker had a second corn picker available. The two machines were identical, and they were the New Idea brand, probably a model 323. This manufacturer had been around for some time, and I trusted the name. I called the farmer and made an appointment to see the machine. It must have sat in the same spot for quite a while because there were three-inch maple saplings growing up through the picker. I cleared all the brush aside, backed up my pickup, attached the picker, and I was away. I couldn't go very fast as this was a fairly large piece of equipment, standing about eight feet tall at the top of the elevator, eight feet wide, and about twenty-five feet long. I had concerns about the stability of the rig when ramping up to highway speeds; after all, the picker was usually towed behind a tractor at less than two miles per hour. I also did not want any road vibration to loosen metal parts, which might become airborne and be impaled into an oncoming vehicle. It must have been quite a sight if you were standing alongside the road watching me pass. There were many remnants of poison ivy,

In These Veins

New Idea Corn Picker

wild brambles, and freshly severed Morning Glory still clinging to the picker, flailing away as I drove down the highway. The picker and I arrived home with no issues.

This piece of machinery had a very strange, awkward appearance to it. It was a one-row picker, possessing several features that would catch the eye of a casual observer. The front had two large parallel sheet metal cones, positioned pointing forward and slightly inclined upward toward the back of the machine. Standing corn stalks would be corralled into the four-inch space between the cones and then ushered into a set of rotating steel rollers where the hardened, dry ears of corn were squeezed from the stalks. The stalk would stay behind, still rooted to the earth. The loose ears were immediately guided onto another set of rollers where the husks were stripped, leaving only the naked, kernelled ear. From there, the ears were dropped onto a long, narrow elevator set at an incline. It featured thin metal paddles welded to a continuously moving flat chain; the chain moved the ears of corn up the elevator while the paddles prevented them from falling back. When the ears reached the top of the elevator, they dropped off into an attached trailer. The entire ensemble was put in motion via a rotating steel shaft powered by a tractor's power take-off (PTO) shaft. This assembly of parts sat on a single axle that rested on two rubber tires, ready to be towed via a long draw bar. Now that I see these words in print, I realize that all pickers look a little strange.

This awkward apparatus would be pulled by a tractor over one row of corn at a time. I thought it must have looked like some prehistoric creature that roamed the earth five million years ago, so I fondly named it the Aardvark.

The season advanced as expected; the plants grew and produced thousands of ears with brightly colored yellow kernels inside. It was time to fire up the Aardvark. The first thing to do was to attempt to locate all the grease fittings, aka Zerk fittings, and protect all the bushings and bearings with a shot of grease. Remember, our Aardvark was from the Mesozoic era and possessed countless moving joints. The absence of grease would lead to a certain failure. I am convinced that I never located all those Zerks. Let's also not forget that our furless beast had not seen any movement in upwards of twenty years. I couldn't be sure what kind of aches and pains it might experience when I tried to breathe life into it.

I hooked the picker up to the Massey Ferguson, attached the four-wheeled trailer, and off we went. Now, I haven't spoken of this yet, but it is immensely helpful to possess a broad knowledge set when entering the agricultural arena. Things like strength of materials, friction, centrifugal force, and vibration analysis all came to mind as I crossed my fingers and slowly put the Aardvark in gear. This machine was a classic example of a true mechanical marvel. There were no electrical circuits, no microchips, no digital displays, no hydraulics, and no safety features! It was just steel on steel, and I knew I needed to take inventory of where my hands and arms were at all times. One distraction could have easily left me with one less digit. The safety manual had disappeared many moons ago and had likely made a wonderful cellulose home for a family of field mice.

I made the first pass, and you guessed right; the Aardvark and I experienced our first breakdown. There were numerous flat chains driven by various sprockets that performed different functions. Once this ancient creature was fired up, it made so much noise that it sounded like something was broken all the time. The only way to know if we were having a breakdown was to look back and see a part with no motion or a massive clump of corn debris. So, for our first failure, the intake chain that guides the stalks into the cob rollers broke. I disconnected the picker from the trailer, headed down to the shop, and utilized one of my recently acquired skill sets, welding. In half an hour, we were back in business. I returned to what seemed like an endless thread of stalks. An hour passed, and then there was breakdown number two. This scenario would repeat too many times to count.

Corn cribs

Did I mention patience in the needed skill set? Yes, this attribute is also needed in farming. I did eventually get the crop picked. I would repeat the whole process the following year, but it ended there. The return on investment was just not to be had. I placed an ad in the Farm Bureau classifieds and sold my antique beast for the same price I had paid for it!

TWO

Frenchie and the Doodlebug

*A story about the poor farmer's
tractor and how one rogue doodlebug
scared the pants off me.*

ON THE WEST END OF THE MAIN STREET IN OUR LITTLE TOWN of Montgomery, New York, where I grew up, my father's one-acre homestead sat opposite a Sunoco gas station called Sloat's Garage. Directly behind the garage was a classic American junkyard—full of worn-out or previously crashed cars and trucks. It was not large but had all the usual features. It was a sea of disconnected colors. Blue, red, green, and white partially raided automobile hulks were scattered everywhere. A color photograph would have made an awesome jigsaw puzzle. Little cramped road paths wound around tiny islands of clustered auto hulks. There were cars with missing trunks, doors, and bumpers. You could always find a loose engine lying deserted on the grass, having been hastily yanked from its moorings with wires and tubes still attached. With permission, one could amble around and over the rusting bodies and often be startled by a darting woodchuck, a screeching feral cat, or the stings from a swarm of yellow jackets. The junkyard age could be gauged by the diameter of a sapling or tree growing through or near a car. Back at the garage, you could get a new set of tires or have a repair made. You could buy gasoline at eighteen cents per gallon, and your purchase would include a windshield cleaning and a brief chat with Mr. Sloat.

Summer days often found me crossing the street to Sloat's office. It was here I would find a small freezer of ice cream and popsicles alongside the cooler of Orange Crush soda and Hires Root Beer. These sweet treats were the highlight of my day when the thermometer was pushing ninety. I will finish this recollection shortly, but I must divert to the chapter's topic, the doodlebug. Starting in the 1920s and continuing through the 1940s, small farms had a difficult time putting enough money together to buy a proper tractor. There was a do-it-yourself alternative called the doodlebug tractor. It began as a modification of the Ford Model T. Later, truck makes and models would also be fair game. There were conversion kits offered at $300, but even this option could be cost-prohibitive. To make a doodlebug, all the sheet metal on the vehicle would be removed, usually sparing the engine hood and dashboard covering. The frame and driveshaft were shortened, and the rear wheels moved forward. Larger rear rims and tires were added, as well as tire chains, to improve traction. The doodlebugs could do a lot of the tasks performed by their real tractor idols, such as plowing, working in hay, and disking. Many farmers had the natural skill set to make the conversion without a kit for little cost.

There was a French national family two houses up from ours. They had a son we all knew as Frenchie, who was about eighteen years old—I never learned his real name. He was five foot ten, had a muscular build, smoked Lucky Strike cigarettes, and walked with a swagger. He spoke with a faint French accent. I was about ten at the time. Perhaps he had a bully trait that we hear so much about these days. Frenchie had one of the aforementioned doodlebugs. I was leaving Sloat's minding my own business one day, enjoying my ice cream cone and root beer, when out of nowhere came Frenchie barreling down the side of the highway, aiming his rusty imitation directly at me. There was no time to react and nowhere to hide. He skidded to a stop just a few feet short of bodily impact. He smiled and chuckled. He just wanted to scare me, and it worked!

THREE

Rabbit Trap

Young boys can be very naive. This story explains my attempt to snag my first rabbit and how it went astray.

My father grew up in a farming family. He arrived in America at five-months-old with my grandparents in 1923 from Holland. My grandfather immigrated here by way of a sponsorship with a man named Peter Hagen, another Dutch national. Peter was in the dairy business.

Fast forward to 1947. My father married my mother. They built a house the next year on an acre in the village of Montgomery. Dad had learned carpentry skills while serving in the Army, helping to rebuild war-torn Germany in 1945. With this new skill, he promptly started Morning Glory Construction Company but was unable to flush the farming DNA from his veins. A few years later, Dad erected several outbuildings on the little homestead property: one for the cocker spaniel kennel, one for chickens, and one, well, I can't say, as it never got occupied. The chicken coop was the largest of the three. Five hundred clucking, red-combed, white-feathered fowl filled the coop. I believe all the materials consumed in the construction of these buildings, perhaps even the nails and except for the rolled asphalt roofing and window screening, were previously used. Recycling building materials was popular after World War II.

As I look back at this time, I realize my father had not done a business plan. He had no MBA and no college at all; in fact, he never finished public school as he left home at age twelve. He never allowed his lack of business knowledge or credentials to keep him from moving forward and putting business ideas into motion.

It wasn't long before our feathered fowl were popping out nearly 500 eggs a day. Egg collection quickly fell on my young shoulders. At age eight, my day began with the daily egg harvest. I scoured the nest boxes, filled yellow rubber-coated wire buckets with pristine white eggs, and hoofed them back to the house root cellar. The root cellar was, just as it sounds, a place to store root vegetables and extend their life. The eggs shared this tiny room with potatoes, carrots, and turnips. It was always damp, poorly illuminated, and not very warm; the air was still and musty. An occasional mouse would scurry into the shadows when the single dim light bulb was switched on. It was there my sister, Jeanne, and I would clean, grade, and pack the eggs. My younger brother, Jan, would have liked to help, but he was only two years old at the time. My mother would then transport the eggs daily in the trunk of our used green Packard to a local broker. There was likely no profit to be made, but at least my father's need to farm was being satisfied.

So now it is occurring to you, why is this chapter named "Rabbit Trap," and what does it have to do with chickens? I'm getting to that. As kids, we watched a bunch of cartoon TV shows. Televisions had just been made available. I probably just watched too many episodes of Bugs Bunny and Ricochet Rabbit, and I decided I was going to trap a rabbit. One of them had traumatized the family garden the previous summer. It was early winter with minimum frost in the earth, but I was still able to dig into it. With a pick and shovel, I produced a hole about three feet across and two feet deep in the ground. I covered it with light branches and hay. The trap was set. I was ready to catch a rabbit. It snowed that night.

The next morning, my friend Donald came over to help me with the egg collection. We were making our way back to the root cellar, kidding about the pretty girl in our classroom, when suddenly Donald disappeared. The trap worked! Unfortunately for Donald and me, it just caught the wrong game, which resulted in scrambled eggs all over the snow. Egg sales were reduced by half that day due to an efficiently constructed rabbit trap!

FOUR

The Art of Sledding

In rural New York State, snow sledding was the highlight of our youthful winter events. I share our infatuation with the simple art of downhill sledding.

THERE WASN'T MUCH FOR A KID TO DO IN THE HUDSON VALLEY on cold winter days in the 1950s. There were no video games or internet. The words semiconductor and digital didn't exist. We were lucky every once in a while to get behind a pinball machine if a parent would drive us to an arcade. We could, however, go skiing, ice skating, and sledding. Skiing required travel and money, and since my parents were usually working and we didn't have much money, skiing was not an option for me. Ice skating had potential since most kids my age had a pair of skates. The girls wore petite, white figure skates with teeth cut into the front to assist them in performing tricks, while the boys had bulky, black hockey skates designed more for speed; neither version was comfortable. There were two ponds in town that froze over for at least part of winter. One was near the center of the village, a hefty walk from our house. It was an abandoned creamery pond and was usually claimed by older male teens playing hockey. The other, we called Baty's pond, was an easy jaunt from the homestead. Our local gang congregated here when conditions were right, and it filled out many of our after-school hours until darkness fell.

Since skiing was for the wealthy, skating held our interest some of the time, but sledding became our go-to wintertime sport, and we didn't have to go far to enjoy it. Our one-acre homestead featured what we felt was a fairly steep hill. None of us had been to Aspen, so we didn't know any better. The driveway steadily rose from the state highway to a brief plateau. Our hill continued beyond the driveway and eventually crested at the dog kennel where Dad had a little side business raising cocker spaniel puppies. It felt like we were on top of a mountain, and in fact, this spot was one of the highest points in our village of Montgomery. We were lucky as we had two different sledding trails to choose from. Both began up at the dog kennel. Our favorite, trail number one, was flanked by Mom's flower garden on the left with two enormous thirty-foot-tall Macintosh apple trees on the right. Near the bottom featured Dad's workshop and, a little further, the neighbor's flat yard and the finish point. If you were feeling daring, you could instead turn left after the Macintosh trees and finish the run going down the driveway. The driveway option was usually not chosen as the state highway was the termination point.

Trail number two featured those same Macintosh apple trees now on the left, a curve to the right (picture sliding here) passing near the chicken coop, and terminating at the corn field, which was hopefully a little ponded up with an ice surface.

I was fortunate to own the Cadillac of sleds, a Flexible Flyer. It had steel runners that curved up in the back and then forward to provide a frame for the oak decking. It had a pivoting wood T-bar for steering and, of course, a rope attached to the ends of the T-bar for hauling it back up the hill. Now, all that was needed was snow.

One could vary the sledding experience by taking different positions on the sled. The natural one was on your belly, head cocked up for navigation with hands clamped onto the T-bar for direction control.

Another was a sitting position, feet on the T-bar, and tensioning the tow rope toward you with both hands to help give you a little torso stability. A variant of this was to go "bobsled" style with one or two additional kids behind you. The rear kids would lock their legs around the person in front just as you would on a toboggan. This would minimize dislocated hips. The person in front would do the foot steering.

Braver kids, future war heroes, and dragon slayers would sometimes stand on the sled positioned near the rear, holding only onto the tensioned tow rope for stability. Steering control was not guaranteed as any attempt to remain upright pulled on the T-bar, causing unpredictable directional changes. Some navigation was achieved by shifting one's body weight, but essentially, it became a straight shot down the hill. This version was not recommended! I was the only one to successfully pull off this stunt, and I only executed it one time. I suspect the other sled riders analyzed the upright ride and deemed it to be a stupid stunt. Any departure of one's boots from the sled's slippery wood deck would only result in a visit to the emergency room!

There was also a variation to the belly version, which featured two kids belly down, one kid on top of the other; we slid down the hill piggyback, with the bottom kid steering. The top kid clamped their hands to the top rail on each side, an antique version of a seat belt.

Keep the piggyback image in mind in this paragraph. We were not satisfied with simply flying down the hill at the lightning speed of ten mph. My future love of physics kicked in, and I didn't even know what the phenomenon was called. I constructed a ramp—aka an inclined plane—in the sledding path about mid-point down the trail. The ramp consisted of a row of concrete blocks at the lower end and a plywood deck. Snow was piled on to maintain a slippery surface. My innocent sister, Jeanne, volunteered for our maiden voyage. I took the base position as she laid on top of me, and off we went, quickly gaining speed as we approached the ramp. Then the runners hit the deck, and we were airborne. We likely gained an altitude of three feet. No one had their Kodak with them to record this historical event. The momentary exhilaration ended abruptly at the landing site. Now, mass and gravity were in play. The mass is my piggybacked sister. And gravity, well, we were three feet above the ground, and the only place to go was down… ONTO MY RIB CAGE. Picture yourself lying on a one-inch-thick board, belly down, with a hundred-pound sack of potatoes on your back, all of which is suspended three feet above the frozen ground by four pieces of rope, and the ropes are severed instantly. I lay on the snow, gasping for breath with the wind knocked out of my lungs. Not a very good feeling! Sledding was done for me that day and for my sister as well, even though she didn't get hurt. On a later day, as you will read, she would not be so lucky. The ramp continued to be used from time to time but never again in piggyback mode.

On any one sledding day, there would be eight to ten kids riding the hill. Those days gave us great joy; they were simple days, and we couldn't have been happier. We would constantly need to adjust to snow conditions; some snows were fluffy, some dense and heavy, and others might be icy. We coped with them all. Often, after heavy sledding, we would get out shovels and toss snow back onto our raceways. Usually, once per winter, we were treated to a ponding effect at the end of our trail number two. A corner of the corn field could flood and freeze over, which created new experiences. You could wrench the sled steering to one side and get into a sideways slide, producing an unpredictable but exciting result, until perhaps you hit the cornfield and ended up with a corn stalk jammed up your pant leg.

The ultimate sledding condition was when there would be snow on the ground, it would rain a bit, and then the temperature would drop. Our little homestead hill was too small to get the most out of that kind of weather event, so we'd slog over to an adjacent farm that had a larger and longer hill. The best sledding days started in the morning.

One cold winter morning, a few of us met up after breakfast and headed over to the big hill. Mother Nature had done her rain thing on a foot of snow the previous night before the temperature dropped below freezing. We could walk on the icy surface, towing our sleds behind, and not break through. Being able to stay on the slick surface was a gift. Once at the hilltop, we galloped off a few steps and then belly-flopped onto the sleigh. The speeds attained were unbelievable. We probably should have had helmets and goggles, but this was the 1950s, and no one worried about safety like they do today.

Sledding after lunch was a little tricky. As the sun warmed the snow's surface, the icy cap was not always able to support us. Occasionally, we experienced sledding without the sled, but not predictably and not by choice. Sixty-seven years later, I can still picture this particular sledding day as if it were yesterday. The age range of our band of kids was likely seven to ten years old, and even though we were young, we did possess some sledding wisdom. We knew the afternoon session would require different tactics.

Knowing that the ice surface would be weakening due to a warming sun, we could no longer run and flop onto our sleds. Instead, we placed our sleds gently onto the crusted snow, then carefully positioned our bodies, belly down on the deck, and pushed off. The sleds quickly reach cruising speeds in excess of twenty miles per hour. We successfully made it to the bottom of the hill on the first-afternoon run. The second run was up; I usually went first, and that's when it happened. I was midpoint at a slight dip on the slope when suddenly the runners broke through the crust, stopping the sled instantly but propelling me sled-less, belly sliding, another hundred feet. My sledmates soon experienced the same fate, which was our signal to surrender the day to Mother Nature's intervention.

Most sledding days simply ended with tired, achy bodies, but one day did not. Jeanne had one of the few sleds without a curved runner rail in the rear, and on that day, her safe sledding record was about to expire. The rails ran to the end of the sled and bluntly terminated. For some reason, Jeanne and a sledding mate exchanged sleds. To this day, it is not clear to me how it happened. There must have been multiple simultaneous sled departures from the starting gate. While descending the hill, the sleds must have gotten tangled. My recollection of the accident is fuzzy, but I do remember pulling a runner from my sister's thigh. The straight-runner sled must have pivoted and begun heading down backward. At any rate, it ended up piercing her leg. She got the necessary emergency care and a good scar story to tell. She proudly showed off her scar for many years to come.

FIVE

Potato Days

My first teenage farm job and the foundation for life it placed under me.

IN THE SPRING OF '61, AT THE TENDER AGE OF THIRTEEN, I landed a part-time job at a nearby potato farm. It was owned by George Hoeffner. He had purchased the farm in 1946. There were about 130 acres under cultivation, mostly with potatoes. The vegetables were all trucked off the farm and sold at wholesale at large open markets. This type of agriculture is called—take a guess, and you're probably right—truck farming. I worked for George's son, Frank, who managed the farm crew. The average wage at that time was $1 per hour, so that is what I was offered. Farm wages had been classically lower than most other businesses. There was no negotiation, not that I had developed any skill at this at thirteen. Everyone else there was getting the same wage no matter what they were doing, who they were, how long they were there, or how old they were, so I had no complaint about my $1 per hour wage. I was excited to have a job and be earning my own money.

The farm was about one mile from where I lived, so I biked

over after school. I had a JC Higgins bike sold by Sears and Roebuck. This classic bike featured a red painted frame, one gear, pedal brakes, twenty-six-inch chassis, all steel construction, and no fenders (my choice). Later, I used my farm wages to buy a Columbia, which was my Sunday and special occasion bike. It was blue, still only one gear, and pedal brakes, but it had a headlight, a speedometer, and a cargo rack, and I left the fenders attached.

Over time, I mastered many positions on the farm. Preparing for the potato planting was one of my first jobs. I was fairly tall and lean with good muscle tone, which would quickly develop further. After all, it was a farm where every task involved physical labor and often featured heavy lifting. In the spring, seed potatoes were shipped by rail from Maine to the nearby Maybrook train yard. Frank and a couple of the farm crew would pile into the flatbed truck and head to the yard to make the transfer. There were no pallets or forktrucks in those days. Every single one of those hundred-pound burlap bags of spuds was lugged from train to truck, one at a time. Once back at the farm, the same one thousand bags were handed off one by one and stacked in one of the sheds.

The fields had to be prepped for planting. When the ground firmed up but was not too dry, Frank got out the plows. Being a top dog, he got to operate the nearly new green Oliver 770 tractor with its diesel motor and 47 horsepower. It may not have been the first year, more likely the second year, when I was given a tractor and plow—and five minutes of instruction. The tractor was a red Farmall Super M, wide front, gas engine with 40 horsepower. This was a big step up for me as I had only driven our puppy tractor, the Cub, at home. The plow was a simple three-bottom on two wheels with a trip rope to lower and raise the plows. I dropped the plows, pulled back on the throttle, and bolted down the row at a whopping two miles per hour, smoke and roar steaming from the stack. This was the first time I was given an important

In These Veins

Oliver tractors

work-related task involving large farm equipment. I felt important, trusted, excited, and happy, all at the same time. Was this heaven? It sure seemed like it at the time.

Once the field was prepped, it was back to the potato shed. Some additional effort was needed to prep the seed potatoes for planting. Potatoes aren't grown from seeds, as one might think, but rather from seed potatoes. A seed potato is physically no different than a potato you buy at the grocery store or farm market. A certain amount of the annual potato crop is set aside to ensure farmers have enough potato "seed" to propagate the next season's crop. This allotment will carry the designation of "certified" to assure the farmer is buying disease- and insect-free "seed." So, how does a potato plant grow? Potatoes have eyes; everybody knows that, but do you know what those eyes become? When planted in the earth, one or two of the eyes or buds on a potato will become a plant top and root into the earth. As the plant grows and matures, it produces a cluster of potatoes, also called tubers, beneath the plant. A potato has many of these eyes, often two to six spaced around the surface of the potato. Only one eye is needed to produce a plant, so to extend the "seed" count, the potatoes were split into four pieces with a simple four-knifed machine, thereby quadrupling the amount of "seed." And yes, there would be a few blanks from time to time. The split spuds were then re-bagged, re-stacked, and ready for planting.

Bagged fertilizer arrived at the farm about this time by a tractor-trailer, and it was then moved onto farm trucks. There were still no forklifts in sight, so each eighty-pound bag was moved one at a time from trailer to truck. I do not know what possessed me to do it, but over time, I was able to move three bags at a time. These were not the bottom three bags in the stack; they were at hip height. It was more like a lateral move and a short shuffle to the farm truck. I didn't do it continuously, but I did do it a few times. A very efficient move in my eyes. I should have asked for a raise.

During my tenure, the farm was using a two-row planter. They would later upgrade to a four-row. The planter was a simple machine but very effective. It was pulled by one of the tractors. Someone sat on the back of the planter, monitoring all the mechanisms and the hopper status. That was my job. Two rotating steel disks split a narrow trench in the soil, and another rotating segmented disk with needles on the circumference would stab a potato wedge that had dropped from the hopper. At the right moment, the wedge was plucked from the needles and dropped into the furrow. A little fertilizer was drizzled into the still-open furrow, and another disk—reversed from the first one—closed the furrow. One hundred acres later, this task was done. Interspersed among the days of potato sowing was the planting of sweet corn which was done with a corn planter. Zucchini squash, snap beans, and cucumbers were planted by hand. Tomato plants were purchased as seedlings and planted with a mechanical transplanter.

IRRIGATION OR PLAYING WITH BIRDS

One of the more memorable tasks was the irrigation operation. New York State receives, on average, forty inches of rain per calendar year, but Mother Nature seemed to be a bit stingy with her moisture during the months of July and August. It was this time of the season when the soil often got too dry to support healthy plant growth. This was our signal to get the irrigation supplies and equipment out of storage.

The Wallkill River, which flowed along the western edge of the farm, provided an ideal, limitless supply of water. Water was sucked out of the river via a six-inch aluminum pipe by a pump powered by a large V8 industrial 1953 Chrysler gas engine. The pump produced ninety psi of water pressure. The engine pumped sometimes for twenty hours straight at full throttle before we would have to break down the pipe setting and move it to a new location. I went with Frank at night a couple of times to monitor the pump. It was easy to see the setup in the dark as we approached because the exhaust manifold was cherry red, complimented by a twelve-inch flame shooting from the stack.

The water was pushed from the pump up a steep hill to a plateau where the potatoes were planted. Pipe had been laid down along the row ends to form a header. Additional pipe was laid in the potato rows at forty-row intervals. A three-quarter inch diameter nozzle Rainbird (we called them birds for short) irrigation mast was placed every 120 feet. An irrigation run was four hours with four birds. At the end of a four-hour cycle, four more birds were turned on, and the initial four turned off. Frank was only eighteen and still had some kid in him. While we were making a bird changeover, Frank occasionally shocked the crap out of me by training one of the active birds in my direction, showering me with cold brown river water. I had no choice but to retaliate with my bird.

HYDRATION

Summers always seemed to be hot on the farm, and we were always looking for our next drink of water. We didn't have to be told by a doctor to keep our bodies hydrated; we were simply thirsty. The water source was a repurposed one-gallon glass wine jug. It was filled with fresh water at the beginning of our morning shift and again just after lunch. It didn't take long in the summer heat to turn the initial cold water to hot, so most of the time, we were gulping down heated water to quench our thirst. Our hydration needs seemed to be highest when we were moving the six-inch by thirty-foot aluminum irrigation pipe in the potato patch. Frank would turn off the pump after a four-hour run, and we began disconnecting the pipe and marching it over forty potato rows to the next segment. The air temperature was usually ninety degrees, and the humidity was higher. It was like being in a sauna and not having to pay for it, although I can't be certain of this as I have never experienced a sauna. The only thing on our minds after an hour of humping pipe was, *Which row was the water jug placed in?* Eventually, someone would locate it, and the hot jug would be passed around the crew, satisfying our pent-up thirst. We always hoped George would take his swig last; otherwise, our quaff would be flavored with Mechanics Delight chewing tobacco.

HAY HARVEST

Part of the Hoeffner operation was raising beef cattle, so ear corn was grown for feed as well as hay. The hay harvest took place once or twice per summer, and of course, only on the hottest days, or so it seemed. We traded services with Frank's cousin John, whose farm was nearby. John cut and baled all the hay, and Frank provided the labor to pick it up on both farms. An intermediate job between cutting and baling the hay was my responsibility. I ran the crimper, a six-foot-wide machine towed by a tractor and powered by the tractor's PTO shaft. It featured two large parallel, cylindrical, rubber-coated steel rollers positioned close together, which drew in the cut hay, crimped the grass's stem, and spit it out neatly in the rear. The intent was to speed up the drying cycle of the hay. Crimped hay enabled the baling to commence sooner.

Once the hay was baled, we came in with our little crew. One person drove the tractor pulling a trailer, two were on foot fetching bales, and one was on the trailer stacking the load. A trailer had a front rack or headboard and sometimes one in the rear as well. The trick was to carefully place each bale so each subsequent row would bridge seams in the previous row. The bales were stacked six high per row. A poorly stacked load had little chance of making it back to the barn. For this job, I was not so lucky as I was assigned to stacking. The bales weighed about fifty pounds each. There was an endless supply of empty trailers; each trailer held one hundred bales. It was classic Hudson Valley summer weather, ninety degrees and ninety percent humidity. One day stood out as my most physically challenging experience; I loaded ten trailers that day.

Stacked high with hay, the trailers sat idle overnight. The next morning, we were assigned loft detail. A long elevator was placed at the loft door high above the ground. A loaded trailer was positioned at the other end of the elevator. If you were fortunate, you got to unload the trailers. Otherwise, you were directed to the loft, which is where I seemed to end up. It felt as though we were being punished for a crime we didn't commit. I don't remember being told my Miranda rights. Even in the morning, the loft was hot, especially when the loft was filling up to the roof. Inside the loft, there was no air movement, the humidity meter was at ninety, and a year's supply of dust could be inhaled into your lungs. A relentless barrage of bales dropped at our feet, and we worked like madmen in what was pretty much a fruitless effort to keep up. It was a sweet sound to hear the silenced elevator when the trailers were finally empty.

It seemed that whenever we got caught up on farm tasks, we were given a hoe and sent out to scratch out weeds the cultivator had missed. As I test my memory, I see that this effort was mostly directed at the tomato patch. There were countless rows of plants, plant after plant. At the start of each row, the field rose a bit, then fell, hiding the far side. As I worked along hoeing weeds, I would occasionally look up to see how far I still had to go. Sometimes I thought, *Does this row have an end?* Hey, I was a thirteen-year-old kid, and I thought, *Is this a test?* Four hours later, the noon whistle sounded, bringing relief and lunch.

LUNCH

Lunch was the main event for the day. We had five hours of our ten-plus hours already in. George, the farm's owner, was married to Tillie, a tall, stout woman of Polish descent and a classic farm wife. The Hoeffners were of German descent. I did not know it at the time, but Tillie, as well as the rest of the Hoeffner family, would become an important piece of who I would become. Their work ethic, honesty, and loyalty were to be aspired to. Tillie's attire was the same each day, with short-heeled black shoes, a dress with an ever-present apron, and permed black hair. She was a devout Catholic and attended church mass every day. Every lunch was a feast. We all had our proper places to sit around a large rectangular table. George and Tilly flanked the head, followed by Frank, then his two sisters, Viny (short for Vicentia) and Balbina, followed by the help, which would be me and possibly one or two other men. The daily menu could include veggies like potatoes, corn, green beans, and beets—always freshly cooked. Proteins could be beef, pork, liver, sweetbreads, even cow brains, and oxtail. And there was always a dish of smear (a farm-style cottage cheese).

Lunch time lasted an hour, and often after we had filled our bellies, there was a little time left to move outside to a large wooden bench. The bench was shaded by an ancient sugar maple and faced the farmyard filled with idled tractors and a small corral occupied by their single Jersey dairy cow. Tillie and her daughters would clear the table and wash dishes. Frank stole a short nap. I would often find myself sitting on the bench with George. He was a man of average height, and he was overweight, but not in the usual sense. He was not fat but just had a large round belly. He was a big fan of chewing tobacco; there always seemed to be a juicy wad of it packed in his cheeks. There weren't necessarily a lot of words exchanged as we sat gazing into the yard, waiting for our lunch to digest. An occasional story was told, which I always cherished. The one I clearly remember had to do with race horses. George's father, Phillip, had a fondness for horses, and in the early 1920s, he acquired a trotter named Justin Brock, who had broken the 2:10 minute mile. Phillip purchased him not to race but to sell his stud service. The love for horses stuck around for a while as George's brother, Bob, bought a one-third interest in a trotter named Darn Fast Horse. When Bob died, George inherited his stake in the trotter. Unfortunately, Darn Fast Horse wasn't all that fast and was sold to a new owner in Sweden.

Doug Glorie

POTATO BEETLES

I was assigned one task that I am quite sure no one reading these words has performed. Insects and diseases present constant time and cost challenges to farmers. Even fast-forwarding to 2023, insects that did not exist in the U.S. twenty years ago now present new crop production hurdles. Nearly all these recent arrivals originate in China and—without intention—are transported via shipping containers. Once here, they find mates and propagate. Insects like brown marmorated stink bugs, spotted wing drosophila, and, recently, spotted lanternflies have become highly invasive and difficult to suppress. Even plant diseases that have been here a long time mutate, and protectants that once worked are now useless. In my potato story, fields were often separated by farm roads. It just made sense from a practical perspective. In this case, the potato beetle population had gotten to the point in one block where no protectant was effective. These beetles start off as small red nymphs, and when adults, become a quarter-inch roundish black and yellow striped beetle. They will defoliate a potato plant in short order. An adjacent block across a roadway had not yet been infested, but there was a migration in progress. There were literally tens of thousands of beetles making the crossing. My task for this afternoon was simple: Drive a tractor down and up the road for the sole purpose of squashing beetles. I did this all afternoon, and by day's end, there were two runny rivers of mud produced by beetle guts and rubber tires. I was impressed by how much "juice" these little critters possessed. This was truly a unique assignment which I am certain none of my classmates had done or would ever perform. I don't know if this was truly effective, but at least an attempt was made. It would have been hard to do nothing and accept the beetle invasion.

SWEET CORN

Sweet corn was also an important piece of the income stream. Different "days to harvest" strains were planted to spread the harvest throughout the summer and into early fall. Corn harvest started mid-summer. Corn picking was kind of an endurance test. Frank trucked us out to the corn patch shortly after 7 a.m. Our daily picking crew consisted of four people: Frank, me, and two others. I use the word endurance because it was summer in the Hudson Valley of New York, where the humidity is often oppressive, or as some would say in our region of New York, "close." (Close is a word that was often used by our family and by others in our town to describe a hot, hazy, very humid day). We were in the middle of a corn field, pushing through seven-foot-tall stalks with a continuous mesh of long, floppy, hard-edged leaves in our path. The corn leaves were just abrasive enough to make tiny cuts on our arms, only to be filled with one's salty sweat. We assembled into two-person teams per two rows. The lead person yanked ears from the stalks with a rapid downward motion, gathered ten ears in the crook of their elbow, and then dumped them into a large paper bag carried by the person following. A bag held fifty ears. A tiny bit of welcome relief was gleaned by way of the morning dew deposited on the stalks, which then was soaked up by our shirts as we moved down each row. Our wet shirts offered a little evaporative cooling. After a very short training period, Frank decided I could lead the crew. There should have been a news article written: "Teen Makes Crew Chief at Local Farm." This was a mini milestone for me, but the thought never occurred to me until years later. I was just happy to be there. Our morning's effort often yielded 400 bags of corn. After lunch, Frank drove the pickup to a nearby town to fetch a load of loose crushed ice. Each bag of corn from the morning pick got a shovel of ice added, and then it was loaded and covered with a tarp for the trip to market.

FARM MARKETS AND SIDE STORIES

Farm markets have been in existence for several thousand years. The players have changed, but the concept hasn't. A farmer brings his product to a space set aside, usually in a city, where buyers can find fresh produce, meat, and cheese. Buyers and farmers banter back and forth for the best price, especially in the wholesale business. Several times a week, the Hoeffners trucked their products to either the Newark, New Jersey, or Bronx Terminal market. I hinted to Frank that I was interested in making a trip to one of the markets. Sometime during my second season at the farm, Frank invited me to ride along to the Newark market. We left the yard at about 3 p.m. with the International flatbed for the one-and-a-half-hour trip with mostly sweet corn on board. This was 1963. Environmental concerns were not a priority then, and when you stop to think about it, every rural town had a dump close by. We must have driven by one of these on the way to market, as the air was hazy and smelled of smoldering garbage. That image of New Jersey stayed with me for a long time.

We arrived at the market before 5 p.m. and got set up. There was a group of islands of steel-roofed canopies, and the farmers backed their trucks into them on both sides. There was a concrete buyers' walkway between the two sides. We unloaded a few bags of corn to make a display, and we waited. Ordinarily, Frank sold the load by early evening and would be back home by midnight. Not that night. By nine o'clock, we had only sold half of our load. The buyers were done for the night, so we were stuck there until morning. We were not about to haul two hundred bags of corn back to the farm. Frank treated me to supper in a nearby bar. I don't think it had been upgraded since the day it opened, likely about 1930. The walls were stained gray from cigarette smoke, and the front glass windows were last cleaned in 1958. Stale cigar smoke lingered in the air. It must have been a slow night as Frank, me, and the bartender were the only inhabitants. This is where I got to have my first beer; I was fourteen, and Mom would never know. It was likely the Rheingold brand. I don't remember how it tasted, but it had to have been great since the legal age to drink it was still five years away. We placed our meal order, and shortly, plates of food were clanked onto the bar. This was not Tillie's cooking! Once our bellies were full, the next question was, where were we going to sleep? We were not about to get a hotel, so I was given the readily available luxury suite, the truck cab seat. Frank got the economy accommodation, which translated to the top of the corn load. We had heard a rumor of a recent knifing incident nearby. I slept with one eye open.

The night passed, yielding to morning and disappointingly light buyer attendance at the market. Frank finally made a sale for the load at half the usual market price, and we headed home.

Frank and I continue to this day to compare stories of the '60s. He recently conveyed one of his many market experiences. It was at the end of a market day, and just like in my story, there was still an abundant portion of corn left on the truck. A woman drove up in a station wagon. They did their price dance, with Frank giving his final price. The woman responded, "If you can get all of this corn in my car, you have a deal." Frank wasn't about to lose an opportunity, and soon after, the wagon pulled away, back bumper scraping the ground.

In one of his farm story recollections, Frank told me of an intoxicated employee who entered the barn one day grumbling about some kind of grievance. He held a revolver in one hand and pointed it at Frank as he marched up to him. Frank was a large, handsome man standing six foot three inches with straight, square shoulders, jet-black hair, and biceps barely confined to his shirt. This was somebody you didn't want to piss off. They exchanged heated words. And then Frank calmly said, "If you're going to use that thing, take your best shot because you won't get another chance." The man stood down, left the premises, and was not seen again.

AUCTIONS

Auctions have been around for centuries and have been heavily used in the agriculture community. It can be an economical way to expand production or simply to fill an equipment need. They were often held in late winter or fall when farmers were less busy. The farmer selling equipment hired an auctioneer and paid him a commission to arrange and conduct the auction. Buyers found out about an auction through ads or word of mouth. In today's world, the auctioneer not only charges the seller a commission but also the buyer. The buyer pays a commission of about five percent. It doesn't seem fair to me.

The auctioneer was always the center of attention at an auction. They seemed to speak a new language, barking loud, stuttered chants of numbers at a rapid-fire pace. Each new number spoken represented a new bid from the buyer audience. During the actual auction, the auctioneer often had an assistant whose job was to spot a buyer's bid. I have been to equipment auctions but am more familiar with cattle. Livestock auctions I attended took place in tiny arenas that could be likened to a small opera house. The buyers' seats were close together, set at a very steep angle, and were too small for most farmers sitting in them, just like at the opera house. The acoustics were usually great, and the space could be used for a small concert except for the lingering odor of that batch of billy goats that passed through the day before. Have you ever seen what adult male goats eat and drink when left on their own? The curious part of the event was to watch the various ways a buyer displayed his bid. Both the auctioneer and assistant continuously panned the crowd. The buyer's signal could vary from a nod, a raised finger, a slow eye wink, a touch of their hat, or, of course, some kind of bark from the buyer's lips. I used the "bark" option as the sales duo did not know my signal. One had to be careful not to have a nervous finger, or an unexpected purchase could occur.

Back on the Hoeffner Farm, Frank needed a potato grader, a large piece of equipment featuring a wood frame, motors, pulleys, belts, and sizing chains. When bagging potatoes, the grader made sure an equal number of different-sized potatoes went into each bag.

An auction was going to be held on Long Island at a farm somewhere east of Riverhead. Frank asked if I wanted to go to the auction with him (I had expressed an interest in experiencing an auction), and of course, I said yes. There were three of us making the trip in the red twenty-foot flatbed International Harvester truck. The Hoeffners seemed to have an affinity for green Oliver tractors and red IH trucks. Charlie, a close friend of George's, was person number three. He would come to the farm a couple times a year to play farm hand. Frank, of course, did the driving, I rode shotgun, and Charlie was in the middle. This seating order was going to have significance.

Now, in Riverhead, we soon found the auction site. It was a "going out of business" auction, so there was a classic display of farm equipment. There were rows of tractors, plows, disks, and harrows. It was the usual crowd of men in oil-stained coveralls and sturdy leather boots with mouths jawing tobacco or sporting a White Owl cigar. The auction started outside and moved slowly, piece by piece; we patiently waited for our turn to bid on the grader. As I write this story now, I think about what goes through the minds of the bidders. The farmer buyer is thinking as he is bidding: *Do I really need this tractor? Does it have a major defect? What is it worth? And is the guy across from me going to keep bidding?*

The auction eventually moved from outside to inside the barn and finally got to the grader. Frank ran the bid up through a couple cycles but decided the price was too lofty, so he bowed out. We went home empty-handed. This was not just a hop, skip, and jump trip, as we were on the road for three-and-a-half hours each way. I don't recall what we talked about to pass the time, but there was a lot of jawing going on. Frank was chewing on his favorite tobacco, Red Man, which was a little sweeter than his father's Mechanics Delight, and Charlie's mouth was loaded with Mechanics. Eventually, one must unload the chew. It was still winter-like, so the windows were rolled up. Without any notice, Charlie leaned over me and disgorged his lethal load of brown nicotine juice, which forcefully splashed against the window glass and then was immediately deposited in my lap. He must have been having a premonition of spring, thinking the window was open. I was partially protected as I was wearing a pair of those oil-stained coveralls previously mentioned, but it was still an unpleasant experience. Both Frank and Charlie broke out in laughter, and I joined in, too!

WORKERS

Seasonal migrant workers are essential to most farms' survival, and since most Americans choose not to work on farms, the U.S. government has implemented an offshore worker program called H2A. A worker is paid a wage set by the United States Department of Labor. The participants are nearly all from foreign countries. The farmer participant pays for the worker's transportation to the U.S. and back to their home country. Workers are provided housing and weekly busing to the store and to a doctor if needed. The program is considered expensive, but the farm at least has a guaranteed workforce. The pool of domestic farm labor is continuously eroding, so this program can be a good option.

The domestic farm worker pool works much the same as it

always has. Workers in this category possess a "green" card, which entitles a non-U.S. citizen to live and work in the United States. Back in 1963, a migrant worker might have started his work year in February in Florida picking strawberries. The migrant received a "piece" rate, so he was paid by the quart or flat for strawberries. When the strawberry harvest was done, the worker may have moved to orange picking. Each farm provided him housing at no cost. So, an East Coast migrant simply worked his way north, picking his way through various commodities as they came into harvest.

The Hoeffner farm hired three to four domestic migrant workers each year. They seemed to show up at the right time for the beginning of the potato harvest in late September. A couple of them were of Puerto Rican descent. Classically, these fellows were lean and short to medium height. One man stands out in my memory. His name was O.C. I am not certain of the spelling as I never saw the name in print, but it sounded like just those two letters. He was a tall black man standing about six foot three and 240 pounds. He had a gentle demeanor and spoke with no noticeable accent, so it is likely his family had been here for decades. He likely came from a long migrant lineage.

Potatoes were planted in mounded earthen rows as the actual potato must be kept from direct sunlight, or they would become green in color. A continuous linear hill had been produced earlier in the season by fat cultivator shoes. The hilling design also facilitated the digging operation. Potatoes were dug by a one-, two- or four-row digger; the Hoeffners had a two-row. It was on two wheels pulled by a tractor and powered by the tractor's PTO or spinning splined steel shaft, which was directly connected to the engine. A wide, flat, steel blade was pulled beneath the hills, forcing dirt, rocks, the potatoes, and their plant over a moving parallel rodded chain. As the chain moved its quarry towards the rear, dirt, and small rocks passed through and fell back to earth. The potatoes and their plant were then deposited neatly on the ground, having been corralled by side chutes. Now, the picker began his day. Burlap bags were laid out along the row. The picker collected the potatoes and tossed them into a thatched basket, which, when full, weighed fifty pounds. The basket was then dumped into the burlap bag, which held two baskets worth of potatoes. The bag was carefully propped vertically in the center of the row to be loaded later. A picker was paid five cents per bag and two cents more if he loaded the bag onto the harvest trailer. The most memorable image I have of O.C. was watching in awe as he loaded the bag. He was able to lift a hundred-pound bag with one arm! O.C. could pick 200 bags per day, and once he met this self-imposed limit, he would leave the field for the day. It did not matter whether there were ten or fifty feet of row remaining; he just walked off.

GUNS AND HUNTING

Hunting game was an integral part of farm life. By their very nature, farms are usually located in rural settings and can occupy ten to ten thousand acres of open space. These open parcels are not only home to cows, corn, hay, tomatoes, or grapes but also provide a habitat for rabbits, pheasants, and deer. Bordering woodlots host squirrels and grouse. During the first three hundred years since the first settlement in 1607 at Jamestown, Virginia, most meat served at the family dinner table was either shot or trapped on one's farm. The need to hunt game waned during the early 1900s as refrigeration gained popularity, but the sport of hunting continues today.

I got my first gun as a Christmas gift from my father when I was twelve. It was a used, twelve-gauge, double-barreled LC Smith shotgun with full and modified choke bores. I never really received much guidance about how to use this gun, so my first shot left an indelible image in my mind and my shoulder. When shooting a gun, one must firmly press the gunstock against your shoulder. The laws of physics tell us that for every action, there is an equal and opposite reaction. This is clearly demonstrated when using a twelve-gauge shotgun. The exploding gunpowder in the shell, propelling the shot forward, produces an equal force through the gun's stock and into the shooter's shoulder. Leaving a space between the stock and the shoulder has the same effect as if someone swung a four-pound sledgehammer at you. I was young then and did not use many swear words, but I'll catch up now, "Son of a bitch, that hurt!"

A couple years later, I bought my first new gun. It was a Winchester bolt action 22 with five and ten shot clips plus a scope. Most people bought their guns from a gun shop, but we had a soda fountain store conveniently located in the village. Howards Luncheonette sold the daily newspaper, coffee, soda, sandwiches, beach balls, and guns. The 22 was great for woodchucks.

Over the span of a couple seasons, Frank and I went after raccoons, deer, woodchucks (every gardener's nemesis), and rabbits. Our usual quarry was the eastern cottontail. Both of us had beagles, which really enhanced the sport. It's hard to explain the feeling I got when listening to the howling canines as they scented out the cottontails. The dogs pushed the rabbits in wide circles in a radius of a couple hundred feet. There was an adrenaline rush as I heard the howls get closer, as I didn't know when or where the bunny would appear, and often I only got one shot.

In winter, with heavy snow on the ground, hunting out in the field became more challenging. We reverted to truck hunting and drove around the back town roads with two loaded shotguns alongside us on the seat. We scanned the road edges for some unsuspecting rabbit nibbling on a low-hanging apple tree. Yes, of course, this was illegal, but we were never caught.

In the spring of 1964, I turned sixteen and felt that, having

Frank and me

worked on the farm for three years, I should get a raise. I had been making $1 per hour during my three years there. I asked Frank if I could have a ten-cent raise, but he said it was not possible. That became the turning point in my young farming career. I ended up working for the local A&P for $1.25. There were no hard feelings. I thoroughly enjoyed my stay at the Hoeffner farm. I never pondered it at the time, but Frank had become like an older brother to me. Frank and his wife, Jane, remain friends of MaryEllen, my wife, and me to this day.

SIX

The '53 Chevrolet

This chapter begins with my lead into my first farm job and then moves to my second year on the farm when I bought my first car at the tender age of fourteen. I wasn't old enough to have a driver's license, but I drove that car all over the farm. Most kids would have a bicycle at this age. I had a car!

I WAS TWELVE YEARS OLD IN THE FALL OF 1960 WHEN I DECIDED to join the school soccer team. As I look back at this time, I can't come up with the reason why. Perhaps a coach asked me or a schoolmate suggested that I should give it a go. I was tall, lean, and muscular and could run like the wind, sprinting the hundred-yard dash in ten seconds, and I would win most of my wrestling matches. With the seed now planted, combined with a few days to germinate, I quickly embraced my decision with gusto. I was going to be a soccer star! I, like every other athlete, had to pass a physical by the school doctor. I had attended just two practice sessions when I received the unexpected results from the physical. The Doc said I had a heart murmur and, right after that, declared that I had rheumatic fever. No soccer for me. Wow, what an auspicious start to the school year. Was this the right diagnosis? I felt fine. Maybe Mom should have gotten another opinion.

The doctor gave my mother instructions to keep me at home, so I ended up missing about eight weeks of school, failing algebra, and, worst of all, I couldn't play soccer. The prescribed treatment must have worked as my heart hasn't failed me yet, although I still have a heart murmur. It was a long eight weeks during which I grew disappointed, disillusioned, and disgruntled about my young life. There would, however, be a positive outcome from this sad period. The same doctor who put the kibosh on my dream of soccer stardom didn't bat an eye when I asked for working papers, and that enabled me to get my first job working at Hoeffner Farm. I ended up working after school every day and on weekends. I eventually added holidays and vacation time. In short order, I had become a thirteen-year-old workaholic. I still couldn't play soccer and never did, but I absolutely loved working on the farm. I couldn't wait to get there every day. I put a lot of speedy miles on my bike, pedaling from home to the farm in eager anticipation of putting in another day of playing—I mean working. I got to drive big tractors and trucks. In the summer, I would bring home fifty and sometimes sixty bucks a week. I had a bank account with money in it. I bought a regulation, slate-topped pool table before I was fourteen. I learned a lot about farming and how to shoot a gun, and I became a skilled hunter.

Sometime during my fourteenth year, an unexpected opportunity came my way. My mother's cousin asked me if I would like to buy a car he no longer needed. Holy cow, fourteen years old, and I could own a car! I don't know why, but my parents said okay. It cost me $250, and the car was mine. It was a beige 1953 Chevrolet Belair sedan, six-cylinder, standard transmission, with "three on the tree." Two shifting versions were available at the time; both had three forward gears and one reverse. Some cars were built with the gear shifter unit anchored to the floor, but this car, like most built that year, had the shifter located just in front and to the right of the steering wheel. The base of the shifting rod pivoted on the steering column. The column represented a tree trunk and the shift lever, a branch, hence "three on the tree." I got permission from Frank to keep the car on the farm and drive on the farm roads.

I had a lot of freedom at fourteen and could do things people would never find out about. The farm roads were fun to drive on, but they were not "official." They were curvy, bumpy, and often muddy after rains or from irrigation overspray, plus they were mostly in view of the farmhouse. The farm I drove on bordered the local county airport. The farm and airport both shared a common side against the Wallkill River. The river area was quite a distance from airport buildings. So, what does a youngster with a car like to do? Yes, go like hell. I was easily able to drive onto the airport property as there were no physical barriers; there may have been "no trespassing" signs, but obviously, I ignored them. The airport had no flight control tower, and the hangers blocked the river view, so no one was likely to see me. The area near the river was flat, so I could test my high-speed skills, and I DID. My newly found raceway, with its mowed grassy surface, was conducive to speed but was scarred with drainage swales every 500 feet to permit water to escape the runways. So, I would swing through all three gears and get up to fifty mph only to slam on the brakes and skid to a near stop to avoid being ejected through the windshield as I neared each swale. There were no seat belts in 1962. I just held tight to the steering wheel; it was great fun. Until today, only I knew about this adventure.

In the fall of 1962, having mastered all the farm roads and having qualified for the Daytona 500 due to my county airport success, I subconsciously must have been looking for another exhilarating experience. I had asked a classmate named Marty to come by the farm and hang out with me for the afternoon. It was late fall, and most of the farm crops had been harvested; a couple of killing frosts had occurred. There was a sweet corn planting located at the base of a potato field—not quite as big as a football field—which had been picked earlier in August and now was just a patch of dried brown stalks. We were tooling around the farm in the '53, always exceeding an imaginary, non-posted speed limit. Without any planning or discussion, I decided to burst the '53 through the corn patch. I drove to the edge of the field, dropped down to first gear, revved the engine, popped the clutch, and off we flew. Cornstalks smacked to the earth, and stalk leaves flew over, under, and through the car with an occasional hardened ear of corn pinging off the windshield. Thirty miles per hour with no visibility until... daylight and the stonewall. No time for brakes. Yes, you guessed it, CRASH, and a little steam rose from the radiator. Our thrilling escapade lasted less than a minute, but nobody got hurt, and it was great fun! The radiator was oozing green fluid, so we were done for the day. I never told my parents about the incident. I just replaced the radiator hose, and we were back in business!

    I never did get over the speed thing. We now have a 1998 Corvette and a 2012 Mercedes Benz E550 with twin turbos, but I don't drive them on airport property or in cornfields.

SEVEN

The Family Garden

*A garden rewards the grower with
a bounty of fresh vegetables and immense
satisfaction, especially when it comes to the daily
summer tomato sandwich. The garden could
possibly be the catalyst for a farming career.*

SINCE MY FATHER WAS BORN INTO A FARMING FAMILY, AS AN adult, I felt compelled to at least try to farm. A garden was a way to keep the farming gene alive. Before we get to the garden, I need to share a little information about my father. He was a long-time alcoholic and made a lot of poor decisions, many of them to do with spending money we didn't have. He carelessly co-signed bank notes for friends and never told my mother, and yet it fell upon her to figure out how to make the monthly payments when his friends defaulted on the loans. My father also had a strong entrepreneurial drive and attempted to seize opportunities, no matter how large or small. This was a time when business plans were not yet in vogue. He quit school at the age of twelve when he left the family nest. Though book knowledge was not his strong suit, his lack of formal education did not dull his quest for a new business.

To illustrate my point, in the heart of winter 1954, there was a snowstorm predicted for the next day. Dad figured if he had a snowplow, he could make some money. He made a deal with a nearby agricultural supply store, and they delivered a red Farmall Cub tractor before dark that same day. Of course, Mom was furious; another note obligation and no way to pay for it. Nevertheless, it became our first tractor. It was a used tractor with a thirteen-horsepower gas engine and a patented quick hitch implement attachment system. As far as farm tractors go, this was tiny; the rear wheels were only three and a half feet tall, but it did what it was intended to do. We only ever had three implements: a mole board plow for plowing the earth, a disk for smoothing the plowed ground, and a snow plow for tomorrow's snow. Dad was likely to make $5 per driveway. I have no recollection of how much money he might have made, but I'm confident it wasn't anywhere near enough to make the first note payment.

I don't know how old I was the following spring. As best I can figure, I was around seven, and I didn't know it, but I was about to be introduced to farming. All my forward motion in agriculture began here. It was spring, and we had some land and a tractor, all the ingredients for a garden, and a start in a farming career. I only remember two things about that first garden day. My father started plowing the garden with our new toy, and I was allowed to finish or smooth the plowed soil with the disk a couple days later. I don't remember receiving instructions or lessons about how to use the Cub, but I must have been told something; after all, this toy had an engine, clutch, and gears, unlike the toy tractor I had pushed around the sand pile the previous August. The other was I learned how not to plant peas. Dad took a hoe, traced a furrow in the soft earth, and then poured a pile of seed into his right hand. Standing over and in line with the furrow, he wound up his arm like a slow-pitch softball pitcher and flung out enough seed to sow half the row. The landed seeds varied in spacing, mostly in the furrow and some not. It must be okay, I thought. He is my father, and this must be the way it's done. I never saw the empty seed package, but it likely said, "Plant seed two inches apart, cover with one inch of soil, and pack lightly."

My gardening skills grew quickly that spring. Dad and I had prepared a large area of soil, large by most any standard, for additional vegetables. Our garden plot measured sixty by eighty feet, the equivalent area of two 2,400 square foot homes. Dad had purchased a bucket of seed packages, including bush beans, sweet corn, radishes, onions, and pumpkins, along with the peas that had been tossed toward a furrow a few days earlier. I don't remember what instructions he gave me, but it seemed that the rest of the planting was now my responsibility. He was off to another carpentry job, and I don't recall that he set foot in the garden for the rest of that season. I continued to be the master of the Glorie homestead garden well into my teens.

I have planted fifty-four consecutive gardens during my life in five different geographic locations in Ulster County. My preferred size has settled down to a thirty by sixty plot, 1,800 square feet—the size of a modest home—containing about a dozen vegetable varieties.

Vegetable gardens can bring enormous feelings of joy and satisfaction. I have never lost my enthusiasm for planning, prepping, planting, and harvesting from my gardens. You may quite likely have one yourself if you live in a rural or suburban environment.

The content of my garden has changed over time. In my opinion—and I'm sure there are some who disagree with me—some plants are just not worth growing, and it is simply easier to get them from the market. Broccoli goes to flower too quickly. Cabbage and cauliflower are easy to grow, but how many heads does one need per season? Brussels sprouts are also easy, but I don't like them. I grew potatoes in the beginning as they are fun to grow. The mature potato ripens underground, so one must dig up the soil to locate them. It's like going on a mini treasure hunt each autumn. My wife's ancestors were mostly Irish, and we use a lot of potatoes in our house; I simply couldn't keep up, so I left it to the professional spud farmer.

There are some vegetables we cannot do without. These are the veggies that only freshly picked will do. Sweet corn and green beans fit in this category. The crown jewel of our garden is tomatoes. We buy seedling plants and get them planted about May 20 when the fear of frost has passed. Most of these are eighty days to harvest, so there is going to be a wait. Nothing seems to happen for two weeks as the plants wait for the soil to warm. Finally, they begin to grow, then flowers begin to appear, followed by a tiny green fruit pebble. A few more weeks pass, the little fruit pebbles grow larger, and some pink coloration appears. Now, we are getting close. It's the longest eighty days of summer. By August 20, we will start picking. Our daily summer lunch diet from now until October 15 is tomato sandwiches. For those of you who have not had a garden-ripened tomato in a sandwich, this is how it's done. A ripe tomato is cut into half-inch thick slices which are placed on toasted bread smeared with Hellmann's mayonnaise; a layer of Vidalia onion is added along with salt and pepper to taste. It wouldn't be summer without our daily tomato sandwich.

MaryEllen, my second marriage soulmate (also referred to as my "second wifetime"), and I now live on our retirement farm in Marlboro, New York. It's now January, and I have all my seeds safely stored in the cellar waiting for spring. I am now seventy-five, and I will still turn the seed packages over to read, "Plant seed two inches apart...". My planting technique does not mimic my father's. I am often asked why I like farming, and I respond, smiling down at my outstretched arm, "It's in these veins."

EIGHT

Black Tuesday

*My sudden transition from a well-paying
corporate career to full-time farming.*

I WORKED FOR THE LOCAL A&P STORE FROM 1964 TO 1968. My stint started in high school, and I left at the end of junior college. My highest wage was $1.25 per hour, and I had to pay union dues. I passed through various positions and ended my tenure as a frozen food manager. In spring of 1966, high school graduation was just around the corner. The store management must have seen something in me, and I was offered a position in the butcher shop, but my mother talked me into going to junior college instead. I finished my two years and got several job offers, but Mom stepped in again and coaxed me into two more years. I graduated from Penn State with a degree in mechanical engineering and landed a position at IBM, also fondly known as Big Blue, in Poughkeepsie, NY. I officially signed on in the summer of 1970.

Many farmers start out having a full-time job and farm on the side. I was one of them. I had a garden at the first house my first wife, Josie, and I rented and then a larger one at our first purchased

Me, building the chicken coop

home. I bought my first tractor, a single-digit horsepower walk-behind Bolens. Wow, I was farming. The Dutch farming gene was kicking in. I was producing veggies for the family, eggs for us and the local fox, and I even nursed a calf to pasture age in our one-car garage.

I never considered myself to be a true IBMer. I wore a jacket or suit, tie, regularly barbered hair, and polished black wing tips, but I always felt a bit awkward in this setting. Give me a hoe, some seeds, and a red sweatband, and I was good to go.

In the spring of 1978, I started to get restless. The farming drumbeat was getting louder, so I went in search of property. I found a sixty-acre parcel nearby. It was mostly wooded and had been farmed at some point in the distant past. The presence of stonewalls always gives a clue. The only structure on the property was a two-story Sears and Roebuck kit house ordered from their

Kids and me with calf

catalog. Sears and Roebuck had a catalog back in the day where one could buy most anything save fresh food. I was very interested in the property but was forced to abandon my pursuit of it when I found that a right-of-way access to the farm was not in order. In late 1978, I found another farm, fifty-four acres. The failure of the first purchase was a blessing in disguise. This new find had a lot going for it. It was a long, narrow parcel on the side of a mountain measuring 800 feet wide by 3,300 feet deep. It started at a 600-foot elevation on the east at the town road, then rose to 850 feet at its westernmost point, ending in woods. The south was bordered by town watershed land and the north by an abandoned vineyard. It faced southeast, looking out towards the mighty Hudson River, a four-minute car ride to its shore. If I were alive in 1609, I would have witnessed Henry Hudson sailing north seeking the elusive Northwest Passage. The farm's orientation provided ample daily sunlight as well as good air and water drainage. The original abandoned house had been lost to fire sometime earlier. Its hillside foundation poked through green ivy along with a few charred, blackened floor beams. A small path behind the house led north to a still intact, gray, two-seater outhouse, complete with a half-moon ventilation hole cut out near the top. Another path, lined with large slate stone, led south to a hand-dug stone-lined well. The property also featured a large post and beam barn circa 1913 with an original metal roof; the original barn had burned sometime earlier. Not far from the barn was a carriage house circa 1852. It took a while to secure an agreement with the sellers, but after a few months of negotiation, we consummated the purchase! My dream to own a farm had come true. We nurtured this property for forty-one years.

In the meantime, I was still at Big Blue. I made my way up the ladder with promotions and raises and became addicted to the Monday morning paychecks. I continued to farm before and after work, weekends, holidays, and vacations. My workaholic initiation at age fourteen went on. Gee, I wonder why my first wife left me?

Tuesday, March 23, 1993, went down as Black Tuesday in the Hudson Valley. This was the day IBM did what had always been unthinkable; they laid off 60,000 worldwide, including 3,000 local employees. On that Tuesday morning, each of the 20,000 Hudson Valley employees was called into their respective second-line manager's office. I knew there was a chance I would be "tapped," as they were calling it, and let go from the company. I was feeling confident and calm, almost happy, and had no worries either way. I had a place to be back on the farm. Perhaps I would be freed from the corporate jungle.

The call came; it was my turn. I locked my office door. My first-line manager escorted me to his manager's office. I knew there were protocols in place for this day. IBM security was on high alert. It was a milestone day in IBM's history. This well-respected

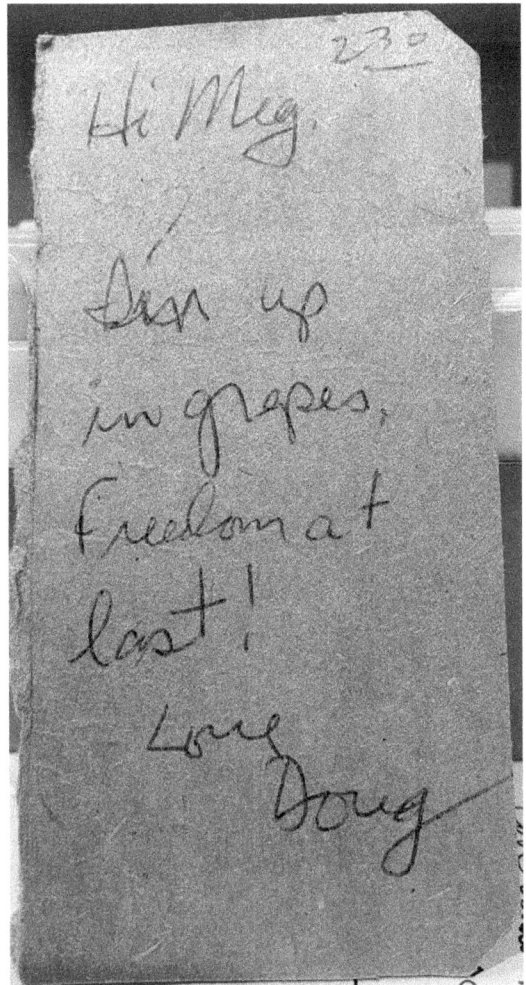

Note to MaryEllen

company had always been a place to have a lasting career, and there were going to be a lot of unhappy people turned loose in the next couple of hours. The manager worked through his spiel, and yes, I got "tapped." Okay then, I knew my fate: Free at last!

My manager escorted me back to my office. I thought, *I am okay with this*. I would only be permitted to stay a few moments, and then I would be officially, physically ushered out of the building. We got to my office door. I fumbled through my pocket to find my key ring and tried to insert the key, but it wouldn't go. "Son of a bitch, they changed the lock already!" No, not really. I was trying to put my car key in the door lock. So, was I nervous? I guess I was. I had been with this company for twenty-three years. I was supposed to retire from here!

By one o'clock, I was in my familiar and comfortable t-shirt, blue jeans, and work boots, working in the vineyard trimming the Seyval Blanc grape block. Freedom and a new life!

NINE

Pay Me One Dollar

An episode in my grandfather's life in Holland that exemplifies the concept of a solid work ethic and personal confidence.

I WANTED THIS STORY TO DEfiNE THE TRAIT OF WORK ETHIC, but it could very well be an example of the art of negotiation or the feeling of confidence.

You already know that my father's father was a Dutch national. He died some forty years ago. My paternal grandfather, Cornelius (Cor), arrived in this country from Holland along with his wife, Anna, and sons, Jan, five months old (my father-to-be), and his older brother, Ellke, in 1923 and was processed at the Ellis Island Immigration Service Center. The business relationship he had with Peter Hagan, the farmer in Sugarloaf who sponsored him, lasted about two years, after which my grandfather started out on his own, renting a dairy farm in the same village. In 1924, Grandpa and Grandma's family expanded with the birth of their first girl, Christina, soon followed by another girl, Anna. Grandpa eventually purchased the rented farm.

During the 1930s, Grandpa dabbled a bit with buying and selling cattle and horses, taking a commission for the service. This effort took him away for periods of time, leaving much of the daily farm work to the four children and Grandma Anna. I believe it was during this time frame that Grandpa developed a wandering eye, which led to the family breakup in 1940. Grandpa then started a new farm in Norwich, NY, taking son Ellke with him. My father had already left the family at the age of twelve to live with the Wright family. I do not know the circumstances that led to his departure. My grandfather sold the farm and then purchased a house in Sugarloaf, NY, for Grandma, where she lived with their two daughters.

My father, mother, and us kids made an annual visit during the 1950s and 1960s to the tiny central New York village of Eaton, where Grandpa eventually landed and lived with his girlfriend, Alma; they never married. Grandpa was a dairy farmer. He didn't trust banks and kept any savings as cash buried in a metal box in the family garden. I recently made my way back to his house, which is now in bad repair, and the village has fewer inhabitants than there were in the 1960s. I was twelve in 1960. I didn't spend much personal time with my grandfather, but I remember him taking me fishing in the farm pond, where I caught a couple of catfish. Later in the 1970s, I took my young family to visit Grandpa. We visited in summer and always sat just outside the back door on a rustic cobblestone patio in the shade of some non-descript tree. Colorful hummingbirds always seemed to visit the red liquid feeder during our chats. He and I sipped rye on the rocks and smoked cheap cigars. He would tell me many stories.

My grandfather was a large man, standing six foot four. He spoke slowly with a mild Dutch accent. It was mesmerizing to hear him speak. He still had most of his brown hair with only a suggestion of gray. His hands were huge. From pinky to thumb, it was twelve inches. I know this to be true as I, too, have very large

Grandpa and me smoking cigars

hands. I just got a ruler out and found that my hands measure ten inches; his were larger. He would deliver one crushing handshake!

Holland is filled with canals, and farms border these waterways. As a youth, my grandfather, likely in his late teens, was employed by a farmer somewhere on the outskirts of Amsterdam. I suspect it was between the towns of Beverwijk and Castricum. The name of the specific town or village is unknown, as my grandfather never told me, and I never thought to ask. I deduced that the farm was located in the Beverwijk/Castricum area because my father was born in Beverwijk, and the family lived in Castricum. I also did a Google Earth search, which revealed that farms continue to exist in this region and most border canals.

One summer day in about the year 1920, the farm workers were harvesting hay and loading it onto a large farm barge in the canal. Once full, the barge was pulled to the barn by a work horse walking the edge of the canal. My grandfather's job for the day was "tender," a person who guided the harnessed horse along the path as it pulled the barge back to the barn. I'm sure he must have performed this routine before. His wage was fifty cents per hour. Grandpa must have felt he wasn't making enough money, so he asked the farmer, "If I do the work of both the horse and the tender, will you pay me one dollar* an hour?" The farmer agreed.

My grandfather harnessed up to the barge and began his trek to the barn. The barge was piled high with hay. Things went along fine for a while, that is, until a breeze kicked up, which made the job a little harder, but he persevered. Then, that breeze increased in strength until it was flat-out windy. To make matters worse, it was blowing from the direction he was headed, and the mounded hay on the barge acted like a ship's sail. The pace he had set for himself soon stalled to a stop. With the wind in his face, the barge was about to drift backward. He dropped to his knees along the canal edge and regained some of his forward motion, but only by clutching bog and reeds in his pathway. He soon resorted to a crawl, inching his way through the mud. He was not about to give up. I've often wondered if, while he was on the ground, the thought occurred to him that he should have asked for even more money, a wage more equal to the task at hand.

I don't remember the end of the story, but I've always assumed he made it to the barn and was paid the one-dollar rate. Does this help describe work ethic? Maybe.

I clearly have a work ethic, but where did it come from? My

---

* I realize that readers who possess a high level of competence in world history and of country currency could challenge the use of "dollar" in this sentence. The Dutch used the guilder as their currency from 1432 to 2002, when they switched to the Euro. This is how my grandfather told the story, and I was not about to correct him.

parents got by and always paid their bills. My father got up every morning and plied his carpentry skills. The family never took what I would call a vacation. Dad just worked basically seven days a week. Is that a work ethic? I think so.

At the age of eight, I was in the rabbit business. As is always the case with rabbits, I started with two, and a month later, there were ten. I would find buyers and make sales. I fed and watered the bunnies every day and cleaned their cages at regular intervals. I stayed engaged in this mini business through high school. Was this the start of my work ethic? Probably.

MaryEllen's nephew and godson, Martin Fox, is an artist. One year, he gifted me a cartoon that depicts me in various activities during a typical day on the farm.

Martin's comic of me

TEN

Firewood

Cutting down large trees can be an exhilarating experience, and at times, the outcome is not as planned.

THE CHAINSAW WAS WAILING AWAY. IT WAS LATE FALL 1979, the week of Thanksgiving, and it was my time to harvest firewood. I had found a seventy-foot tall, fifty-year-old black oak tree measuring twenty-four inches in diameter located in the middle of a ten-acre woodlot. I had carefully placed a notched cut on the east side so the tree would fall to the east. The tree was straight, leaning a little bit to the east, so I felt comfortable and safe that the tree would fall where I intended. As I continued my cutting, now from the west side, the tree began to move and pivot toward the east, at first very slowly, then gaining speed, and after a few seconds, it fell crashing to the ground. Leaves, small branches, and dust filled the air, and then the tree became silent. The tree's first movement from vertical to the last leaf shutter as it reclined on the ground took about twenty seconds. My blood pressure returned to normal. Gravity had done its job and taken the tree down as planned. I am a student of physics, and many tasks that I have tackled in my life have gone more smoothly due to my knowledge of physics. This tree was a perfect example of physics in action.

All trees are not created equal. I used to cut trees that were dead or nearly so, but I found working with live trees to be more predictable. Live trees would more often fall where you wanted them to and more likely enable you to match your life expectancy. Dead trees burn more readily but would often be hotels for black carpenter ants and powder post beetles. Too often, I would hear, "Honey, what are these black ants doing on the kitchen counter?" Live trees classically don't make good housing for insects. The "honey" statement would then lead to the $250 visit from the bug guy.

This oak tree, which I talked about above, was cut from a woodlot that was sold to us as part of the farm that we purchased in 1979. Wood has been used to heat homes, cabins, teepees, and caves since the discovery of fire. I have always liked the idea of being able to be somewhat self-sufficient, and the use of firewood fits this perfectly. Now, when we were looking to buy this property, we were given a copy of the deed for our inspection. A problem arose because the woodlot was not mentioned at all in the property description in the deed. When we questioned the sellers, their reply was, "This property has been in the family forever, and no one has ever challenged us." I was worried that someone could come along later and say, "Hey, that's my property. You can't cut wood off it." So, when I had the property surveyed to satisfy the bank, I asked the surveyor if he could include the woodlot in the deed description. He said, "What do you have to prove that it is included?" I didn't have any proof at the time, but I am not a person who gives up easily when going after something I want, and I did want this property. I decided to do some research at the county office of records, and by looking at the various deeds surrounding this property, I was able to locate the key parcel owners. I contacted each one and got them to agree to meet me at the woodlot with the seller and the surveyor. These adjacent landowners pointed to their respective property corners, all of which, when connected, would outline the boundary of the wood lot in question. This would prove to be enough for the surveyor to certify the inclusion of the woodlot, and we bought the property.

I have always enjoyed cutting firewood. In the early days when I worked for IBM, I would always set aside the week of Thanksgiving to go up to the woodlot and cut the wood needed to satisfy our heating needs in the house for one winter. I always cut wood two years ahead of when it would be needed. Well-cured wood burns the best. We built a new house in 1983, and this was done sometime after the energy crisis of the mid-70s. Picture long lines at the gasoline pumps and high prices for home heating oil. So, when I designed the new house, it included a wood boiler that sat alongside the oil boiler. The idea was to keep the wood boiler hot enough so that the oil boiler simply wouldn't fire and, therefore, not use any oil. Thirty-seven years later, the system still works exactly as it was designed. There was a feeling about having an inventory of firewood—and, in my case, I would have about ten cords on hand all the time—that gave me a sense of a little independence.

We, in fact, used wood extensively to heat various structures on the farm. If I counted them all up, there were five different wood-burning devices that we used to produce heat. We had one in the tasting room of our winery, one downstairs in the barn, which kept the workers warm when they were packing apples in the winter, and one in the shop in a building we call the carriage house. We had a fantastic fireplace in our house and, of course, the wood-burning boiler which I mentioned earlier. There is simply something about being around the stove or a fireplace that burns wood that feels so good.

Oh, by the way, not every tree I have ever felled has gone in

Firewood stack and me

the intended direction. I had planted a new vineyard in a field we called Oasis. The east end of the vineyard was shaded by a sixty-five-foot red oak. Of course, I couldn't deal with shade, as it's counter-productive to ripening grapes, so I decided the tree had to go. It was a very straight tree, which I expected would be easily persuaded to fall to the west, away from the AT&T communication line that dissected our farm. They had a right-of-way across this section of the farm. I picked a day with light winds as the wind can influence the direction the tree will fall. I made a notch on the west side of the tree and began my hinge on the east. I was most of the way through with my cut when a little breeze showed up, and voila, the saw blade got pinched. Okay, no worries, I have been here before. Now, when this happens, one must go to Plan B. I jumped into the pickup and flew down to the barn to get a couple of wedges and a sledgehammer. A couple of good smacks on the wedges in the saw cut should take the tree back to the intended direction. By the time I returned to the scene, the situation had turned ugly. The tree's hinge had given way, and the tree now laid on the AT&T line. This was trouble. The force and weight of the tree snapped off the first AT&T pole just north of said accident scene, and it was dangling from the AT&T line. The next pole just south of the tree was leaning heavily to the east, and two poles to the north were doing the same. At least the chainsaw came free when the tree fell over. I assessed the situation. With a degree in mechanical engineering, I understood forces and physics, but this time, gravity was not my friend. This was a large tree, and it had placed a tremendous amount of weight on the phone line. The supporting steel cable line now had a gazillion pounds of stress on it. I strategically cut branches from the felled tree one by one. Then, I worked the top back toward the middle, where the tree was resting on the cable. I then cut the tree bottom in pieces, still working toward the tree middle. Don't forget about the gazillion pounds of stress. It was still pent up in the final main trunk of the tree, resting on the steel cable. The supremely stressed cable wanted to send the last piece of oak to the moon and perhaps take my head with it.

 I continued to ponder the physics, making carefully calculated cuts with an eye on where and when the final piece of wood would be propelled by the cable. Finally, when enough weight had been removed to tip the scale in favor of the cable's pent-up power, the cable sent the tree trunk flying and freed itself. It left the broken pole—still attached to the cable—dancing in the air and, much to my relief, my head still attached to the rest of my body. I later contacted AT&T and told them a tree had fallen on their line due to a heavy thunderstorm and that I had cleaned up the debris, but they'd better get over here and take care of the damaged poles. No one needed to know the truth.

 Part of the fun of gathering firewood is deciding where in the woods trees should be harvested. To me, harvestable trees should be more than sixteen inches in diameter, leaning, crooked, and of oak species. It is also helpful if the "ripe" trees are clustered and accessible for efficiency purposes. I leave the straight trees alone, thinking they will make good seed or mother trees to provide for future new growth. Access to the woodlot was by way of farm roads and passage through another small stand of woods opening to a peach orchard. During the summer of 2012, I was searching for something to do during a visit from my grandchildren. Perhaps it would pique their interest to leave a little of themselves in the woods? It was in this small section of woods next to the peach orchard that we would do some tree trunk carving. I selected a smooth surfaced maple tree, about ten inches in diameter and thirty feet tall, for each grandchild, Anna, Teah, Cody, and Trey. I gave them a quick lesson on knife safety. Soon, there were four trees, each with four letters and four numbers etched into them. Today, eleven years later, they can find a little of themselves embedded into four fifty-foot-tall maples.

ELEVEN

Another Broken Rib

Farmers are quite prone to being injured. This chapter talks about some of the unique ways I have broken my ribs.

FARMING IS THE SEVENTH MOST DANGEROUS OCCUPATION. I guess when you see the rating, it doesn't look too bad. Anyone working in the agricultural field will likely have had a close call or worse. I have experienced numerous injuries during my farming career. Many of those injuries have been cracked ribs.

When we first took possession of the farm, the soil's agronomy status was unknown. Soil tests were performed, and the results showed a low pH. Most fruit crops like a pH between 6 and 7. In our area of town, the natural pH is about 5. The number is moved up by adding lime to the soil. Soil with a low pH could be called sour; adding lime can "sweeten" the soil. Lime can be spread via a special truck with a spinner on the back. We decided to start by sweetening up a field we called Oasis; ten tons of lime was scheduled. There were no easy access points to the targeted field, so I had to create one. A stonewall, wood posts, and barbed wire had to be removed. The stone tested my back, but it held up fine. Unexpectedly, it was one of the cedar posts that did me in. I was clamped on to one of the posts, and on an inward thrust, it snapped off and, with full force, slammed into my rib cage. I could hear and feel the crack instantaneously. Rib breaks are painful, and recovery usually takes four weeks. While you are on the mend, you want to avoid breathing, laughing, and, most of all, sneezing.

One of the sources of farm revenue in the beginning was the sale of freezer beef. Early on, we bought two-day-old calves in the fall, bottle-fed them indoors through the winter, and turned them out to the pasture in the spring. Eighteen months after purchase, we slaughtered, aged, and custom-cut the beef to our customers' specifications.

Some of the steers could get quite large and reach 2,000 pounds. Most of them were generally quite docile. I don't know why, but occasionally, they would become very frisky. Perhaps a momentary flare of testosterone? Be mindful these are steers; they have no balls! Once one got to jostling and bucking about, invariably, they all joined in. Then, there were ten bovines and thus ten tons of beef on hooves doing their version of the Irish jig. On this particular day, they caught me off guard. Here they came jammin' down the hill at dusk, kicking, bucking, heads thrusting side to side with snorts and snot streaming from their noses. You would have thought you were in a rodeo, but there were no riders on their backs. A matador may have come in handy about now. He didn't mean it, but one of them got me. I don't think he even saw me. I was knocked to the ground windless, with a familiar pain shooting from my rib cage.

There were a couple more rib events, but I will skip to 2017. We grew about three acres of apples, which came to about 1,400 trees. Each tree was trimmed every year. Trimming an apple tree invigorates the tree to produce new fruiting wood. It also enables light and air to get into the tree, which naturally suppresses disease and insect pressure. This trimming process, which could be termed pruning, is done in winter when the tree is dormant or sleeping. I could have delegated the task to others but chose to do it myself as I liked to trim trees. Even though our apple planting was small, it took me about a month to get over all of them.

This orchard was over twenty years old, planted on a dwarfing root stock, in this case, Malling 26. There has been extensive research done during the past hundred years targeted at shrinking the size of an apple tree. Malling is the name of the research station in Kent, England, where experiments were performed to reduce the size of apple trees. Apple tree rootstock refers to the lower part of an apple tree onto which a different apple variety (the scion) is grafted. Different root stock selections yield a variety of mature tree sizes. Malling 26 yields a mid-size tree. Economic studies have shown that increasing the tree density—the number of trees you can plant in an acre—yields higher profits. I tried to keep our trees at about twelve feet tall.

I had been trimming trees for many years and had ascended and descended a ladder probably 10,000 times. I had always felt that music helped me get this task done more quickly. Unlike some other places on the farm, this orchard had good FM reception; I had my radio headset clamped over my ears. I was tuned to my favorite station, WKZE, which plays an awesome range of eclectic music. I had been known to sing along perched at the ladder's top rung. It was a cold day in January, late in the afternoon, heading towards dusk. The ground was bare and frozen.

I was making a routine limb cut. I usually locked the top of my right knee against the bottom of the next rung up from where I was standing, which tended to keep me in place. I must not have done this for this cut because, for no apparent reason, I lost my balance and, within what seemed like one heartbeat, fell squarely on my left side onto the frozen earth. I have practiced falling gracefully over the years, but that was not what happened that day. I laid on the cold, hard ground for five minutes while my brain assessed the body for damage. Reports were coming in. Report number one, you have likely torn ligaments in your left hand. Number two, you have some trauma in your hip, may be fractured. Number three, one or two ribs are cracked. A couple more moments passed, and I concurred with my brain.

I slowly got my feet under me. Now, here's the stupid part. I asked myself, *Am I going to be able to trim trees in the morning?* Even at sixty-nine years old, it was hard to shake the workaholic routine. I tested myself and attempted to climb the ladder. The answer came back, *You're not trimming trees tomorrow.* I slowly limped to the house, calling MaryEllen on my way. She met me near the car and drove me to the local emergency care facility. Several x-ray scans later, my suspicions were confirmed. Torn hand tendons, bruised hip, and, of course, cracked ribs. The body mended itself, and I awaited the next acrobatic mishap.

The broken rib mending process, although not horrible, does present challenges. The simple event of rising from the bed or recliner causes darts of intense pain in one's chest. MaryEllen attempted to be her helpful self by lending a hand and a tug. After a few spousal assists, I suggested to MaryEllen that she move to another room and simply let me curse my way out of the chair. I did learn a new way to get out of bed with minimum pain, which I have used every day since.

TWELVE

Stone Walls

*These carefully crafted structures
are more than just piled rock.*

OUR FARM WAS IN ULSTER COUNTY IN NEW YORK STATE. I AM not certain when our area was first settled, but there are houses in nearby New Paltz and Kingston that have dwellings dating back to the 1770s, and two local farms go back nine generations and two hundred years. I guess our farm began its life sometime in the early 1800s. This farm was located in what's locally known as the Marlboro Mountains. It is part of the Hudson River Valley, which was formed some 10,000 years ago during the glacial period, so there are lots of hills, mountains, cliffs, and rocks. The land was naturally forested with deciduous and conifer trees. Early settlers cleared the land to create fields for grazing domestic animals. As the land was cleared and worked, tens of thousands of tons of rock were unearthed. The stone was moved by men, horses, and stone boats (a flat wooden platform towed by horses). It must have taken many thousands of man-hours to get the rock off the land and stacked onto the borders of the property, as well as many interior stone walls. Each field on the farm was about three acres big and surrounded by stone walls. I suspect that the owners of the property at that time simply hired people who wandered onto their farms. They probably paid them a dollar a day and gave them "three hots and a cot." I have always wondered what the stone walls really represent. The obvious was that it was a place to put stone. Secondly, it became a visual cue so you and your neighbor would know where your borders were. Land deeds in our area often refer to stone walls as the official/legal property boundary. The stone walls additionally created natural barriers that would keep the livestock from wandering off.

Lastly, another aspect of having walls on the property was that over time, due to frost action and the weight of these walls, the walls would sink into the earth a bit and produce a sunken profile along the wall footprint. When this happened, especially in the spring, when there was an excess of water in the soil from spring rains and the snowmelt, you could hear water, seemingly underground, following the stone wall. The walls became an integral part of the farm drainage system.

Wall design was very consistent across our geographic area. Shale is the dominant type of stone found here, which made it quite easy to construct walls with as it is a sedimentary type of rock that often naturally breaks into sheets two to six inches thick, which facilitates the stacking of stones one on top of the other. Walls were always built wider at the base and narrower at the top, which reduced the likelihood of them falling over. The width at the base varied from three to five feet, but there were some on our farm that measured ten feet wide. The fatter walls were always near a field that contained more rocks. The construction of any wall started by placing outside rocks first. Smaller rocks were placed on the inside as the rock sides grew in height. Most walls topped out at four feet and were capped by large, heavy, flat stones. There were instances on our farm where the original

Stone wall stile

farmers added a little flare to their design by integrating flat, protruding step stones, called stiles, into the side of a wall to permit easy access over a wall. As a testament to their strength and durability, I imagine many of our stone walls look the same as they must have two hundred years ago!

Over the last forty years, I have driven by and walked these stone walls thousands of times, and I've often wondered what they have seen and heard. Countless animals have crossed them, sat on them, stored nuts in them, and lived in them. They've seen rain, fog, ice, hail, and snow and have lichen clinging to them. The walls represent a link to the past as well as a tranquil grounding image in one's viewshed. They have heard somebody singing a song or whistling a tune or a farmer cursing because the horse wouldn't move fast enough.

We live in a world where the extremes of nature and geo-political

Stone wall

strife shake our feeling of stability from time to time. To me, the walls symbolize a sense of security and reliability. Our farm's walls have endured for two centuries and will likely remain for many years to come.

THIRTEEN

Barn on Fire

*Structure fires rarely have a good outcome,
but this one turned out okay.*

IT WAS SUMMER 1985, AND THE SUNLIT DAY WAS QUICKLY moving from dusk to dark. I was preparing to apply a tank of crop protectant to a peach orchard. This was very early in my farming career, and we didn't have any modern equipment. I had an engine-driven three-piston Hardie sprayer, a hundred-gallon capacity, circa 1940. I was pulling it with a 1958 Massey Ferguson model 50 with a gasoline engine. The sprayer was old, but it could still produce a lot of water pressure. I used a handheld spray gun to apply the protectant, aiming it at each tree as I passed. Once the tractor was gassed up and the sprayer was filled, it wasn't just a matter of hopping on the tractor and heading out to spray the trees. First, I had to don my spray "uniform." To look at me, you would think I was preparing for the next lunar landing. The protective outfit included a rubber rain suit, rubber boots, rubber gloves, goggles, a charcoal-filtered mask, and protective hearing muffs topped off with a wide-brimmed waterproof hat. In future years, we upgraded to cab tractors, which inherently protect the operator from spray drift while also saving me a lot of time and discomfort.

The peach orchard sat high on the mountain about 400 yards west of the "yard" area. At the time, the farmyard included our house, a large circa 1913 barn, and the carriage house.

As I sprayed up and down the peach tree rows, I had a view down the hill, looking east toward the yard, across the street, and the entire Hudson Valley below. At one point in one of my circuits, an orange glow caught my eye. *Holy shit, the barn's on fire!* I didn't have a cell phone; this was 1985. I couldn't drive the rig down the hill; it was just too slow. Plan B, RUN! In a matter of sixty seconds, I got the tractor stopped, two engines turned off, goggles, snorkel, and muffs tossed, and away I went, practicing the hundred-yard dash I was so good at in high school. The knee-high rubber boots were clearly not an asset. I ran as hard as I could, thinking, *How did the fire start, and why isn't the fire department here?* As I was getting close to making my final descent toward the orange barn in front of me, the hill turned very steep, and I began to lose my vertical stability. The top of my body was moving ahead of my feet. I have always prided myself on being a good "faller." So, I went into my tumble routine. After numerous revolutions, I found myself upright once again and peering at—and somehow through—the barn. It didn't make sense at first, and then my brain figured out what my eyes saw. The barn was NOT on fire! It turned out that my neighbor Jimmy, across the street, was doing a late-day brush burn. Our large west barn door was open, and I was seeing his fire through the east barn window. What a relief!

FOURTEEN

French Drains

*The concept and practice of draining
soggy farmland has been around for thousands
of years. I describe the function and durability of
French drains on our farm.*

FRENCH DRAINS HAVE BEEN USED AROUND THE GLOBE FOR thousands of years. I haven't a clue as to how the French got dibs on this drain. In its basic form, it is simply a gravel-lined ditch in the earth. They are very useful in moving groundwater away from a place where it wants to stagnate. My observations on our farm told me that these covered ditches are two to three feet deep and about the same in width.

My first encounter with a French drain was when I observed water overflowing from the barn well. The water left the well rim and quickly disappeared into a stone conduit, then reappeared 300 feet away across the driveway. Technically, this was not a French drain, as it was transporting water and not removing it from the soil. Maybe I had discovered an Italian conduit. Or an Irish conduit. It couldn't be American. Our country is not old enough to make these claims. I had reason to uncover this conduit about ten years ago. I had damaged it while ripping the soil for a new apple orchard. Once I enlarged the damaged area to make a proper repair, I was amazed at the durability of the drain's design. Flat rocks had been placed at the bottom as the surface for water to flow over. The sides were flanked with twelve-inch square-sided stone. The top was crowned with a series of flat stones, creating a bridge across the two sides. I know, I know, how does this man get so excited about this simple stuff? The thing is that this conduit was put here 200 years ago, and it was still in perfect condition, doing what it was designed to do. Look up from this print. Do you see anything in your vision field that is manmade, 200 years old, and still works perfectly? You're lucky to get ten years from your computer or hot water heater!

During our turn to own this land, I located more than twenty French drains distributed throughout the property. Nearly all of them were functioning. I would usually find them when adding an irrigation line, erecting a building, or adding more drainage. All of those that I encountered were of the same simple design. They were always about three feet deep, with eighteen inches of mostly small stone lining the bottom. Earth covered the stone. I ponder how much effort it took to produce these little marvels; there were no excavators or bulldozers; it was all done with strong backs, shovels, horses, stone boats, and countless man-years of effort. Soil drainage design improved with the introduction of clay tiles in the mid-1800s; tiles have been used in Scotland since 1810. Their design resembled a pipe with an inside diameter of four inches by eighteen inches long. Tile pieces were laid end to end at the bottom of the field trench, thereby providing a conduit for groundwater to easily exit a wet field. I suspect tiling was not used on our farm due to the extra cost of the tile. The term "tiling" stuck and is still used today. The clay conduit design has now been replaced with plastic, usually available in 250' long coils.

Our farm was long and narrow, measuring 800' wide and 3,300' long. The long dimension ran in an east-west direction, covering a 250' elevation change. There were no flat areas, save the "barnyard" on the farm. It boasted of ample air drainage, which was great for mitigating spring freezes. Rainwater on the soil surface tended to move down the mountain quickly, yet there were areas on the farm where fruit trees struggled to grow in overly moist soil. Fruit trees do not like wet feet. Most of the soils contained a lot of clay, which has a propensity to hold water. In some areas, when plowing in preparation for new planting, the soil was the color of Gulden's mustard. During wetter times of the year, the clay soil could easily become saturated. This is the same soil zone where the tree roots live. Saturated soil inhibits the roots from "breathing" and often kills the tree.

All this agricultural drama can be avoided by adding strategically placed French drains. As I explained earlier, another term for this process is tiling. Over the years, we added several thousand feet of tile. Our design was to dig trenches one foot wide by thirty inches deep, place four-inch perforated HDPE pipe on the bottom, fill the trench most of the way with ¾-inch stone and dress the top with soil. Orchards and vines planted in these areas never experienced growing issues.

FIFTEEN

The Massey Ferguson

*The story of the life of our first farm tractor.
It was the only one we had in the beginning,
and it often tested our mettle.*

OUR FIRST TRACTOR WAS A 1958 WIDE-FRONT MASSEY FERGUson. It had a gasoline engine, 38 PTO horsepower, two-wheel drive, three forward and one reverse gear with 12.9 x 24 rear tires. I know this is a lot of detail, but some people reading this want to know, especially farmers, as they are always comparing tractor specifications. I know I would. I bought it used for $2,500 in New Paltz, NY, in 1979. This would be the only tractor I had for the first five years. This tractor could perform all the machine tasks on our farm. These included plowing snow and pulling the manure spreader, corn picker, firewood trailer, field disk, spring tooth harrow, and fruit trailer. Its three-point hitch carried the cultivator, two-bottom moldboard plow, brush hog, sprayer, or fertilizer spreader. It was the heartbeat of our young enterprise.

At our peak, we had six tractors: a Ford Orchard 4000, a John Deere 2150, a New Holland 4430, a New Holland TN70, a John

Deere 5083EN, and a New Holland T4-90. These were all powered by diesel engines. Diesel engines are more reliable than those powered by gasoline. The benefit of having multiple tractors was that each one was matched and dedicated to a particular task. I could keep a tractor hooked up to the same piece of equipment for a long period of time, which saved the effort and time needed to hook and detach implements.

The need for a tractor during our first season was largely driven by the need to plow snow, which would arrive in December. But the tractor's real worth would show in the spring. This was the prep time for planting. The Massey's very first job was to plow a three-acre field in preparation to sow corn seed. The field had at one time been used for hay and pasture, and I don't think it had seen a plow in fifty years. There was a high probability there would be a confrontation with some rock; after all, this is Marlboro. I only had a two-bottom plow, so this task was going to take a while. The tractor and plow were only going to travel at one-half mile per hour, and I was only able to turn two feet of soil per pass. I made three passes and then encountered my first breakdown. The throttle had suddenly become useless, with no control over the engine's RPMs. I was about to learn about "governors." I knew states had governors but not tractors.

A governor is a mechanism that allows the throttle to be set at any desired RPM and, therefore, the speed of the tractor's forward movement. A broken governor equals no movement. I placed an order for the necessary parts, and they soon arrived. The process of repairing a governor was completely foreign to me, but having a mechanical degree proved helpful, and it turned out to be not that complicated. I lost a couple of days and got back to plowing. Turning the soil over is one of those farm tasks I have always enjoyed. The soil surface starts out green with grass and then instantly changes to brown with dirt. After a day's effort, the three-acre field was all brown. I just did something, and I could see what it was. The farmer gets continuous feedback about his accomplishments. The field now had 500 furrows sliced across it, and although the result was nice to look at, it was not yet suitable for planting. Out came the disk to smooth it over. Again, with each pass, I could see exactly where I'd been. I was getting visual feedback on my progress. The tasks continued with a spring tooth harrow pass and, finally, the planting of the corn. For each step in the process, I was rewarded with a sense of accomplishment. This is one of the primary reasons why I farm. I am lucky to be part of this tiny group of Americans engaged in agriculture. I love to farm! Today is March 3, 2023. I turned seventy-five today, and I can't wait to get outside to trim an apple tree.

Farm tractors are unique mechanical machines. They tend to last a very long time. Your lawn mower may give you ten years, and your car perhaps twenty, but farm tractors go fifty years and more. Consider the Ford 9N. It was first sold in 1939 for about $1,400. These same tractors are still used today and still sell for $1,400 or more. Another intriguing aspect of the farm tractor is its horsepower rating. Technically, horsepower is the rate at which work is done or Force x Distance divided by Time. Consider that most of the tractors sold in the '40s and '50s had less than 50 HP. A '57 Chevy with a 265-cubic-inch engine had 162 HP. How can you explain the big difference? You would think that the tractor would have hundreds of horsepower. After all, its sole purpose in life was to do WORK. Well, it's all in the gearing. The Chevy was designed to go at a hundred mph and still have a little torque left. The Massey was designed to travel and be able to pull something at two mph. The horsepower gets compressed through its gearing, so buckets of engine HP are simply not needed. There is a more technical explanation, but then you are going to put this book down if I keep going.

We began to outgrow the Massey's abilities in the early nineties. One winter, we had a particularly heavy snowfall all day and into

Massey Ferguson 50

the night. I waited until the next morning to move the snow. Incredibly, we had gotten about thirty-six inches. In hindsight, I should have gone out at 11:00 the previous night to push some of it aside, but who wants to go out into twenty-degree temps with wind and no cab on the tractor? Our driveway was 800 feet long and all uphill. I started from the top and worked my way down toward the town road. I believed I was prepared, having applied my set of two-inch link chains on the rear tires. On my first pass down the driveway, there was some drifting near the bottom, and now the snow was dropping over the top of the plow. With the Massey's rear wheels spinning, all forward motion ceased. I tried backing up to no avail. I was stuck. I had a flashback to catalog images I had been viewing during the last couple of months. Images of four-wheel drive shiny new machines with cabs and HEAT. I trudged up the hill through the poorly plowed roadway to fetch a shovel. It seemed a little odd to need to shovel out a snow-plowing machine. I decided to take a short break to thaw my frozen fingers. I stiffly shuffled into the basement; the eighty-degree wood stove heated air felt really good. Shortly after, I got the tractor freed up and eventually finished the task. The seed for a tractor with a cab had been planted.

It was not too long after the snow plowing incident that Massey signed its death warrant. It was performing some nondescript task when its governor failed again. Remember, a governor is the mechanism that stabilizes the engine's RPMs. No governor equals no RPMs. This was the third time this had happened. I headed back to the house and, upon entering the kitchen, threw my cap across the table, uttering the usual expletives. MaryEllen responded with, "Maybe we should try to get a new tractor." Soon after, we analyzed our finances and decided we could do it. We traded the Massey in when we purchased the New Holland 4430 with a climate-controlled cab. I suspect our '58 Massey is purring along on some farm somewhere. We never saw it again.

SIXTEEN

Farm Dog

Farms and dogs go together like apple pie and ice cream. We have had several dogs at our farm over time. One eventful day tested our emotions.

I SUSPECT THAT MOST FARMS HAVE A DOG. DOGS ARE LIKELY the most popular pets on the planet. They are always cheerful, and all they want to do is please their owner. Farm dogs have it a little better than their city brethren. They have more land to roam on, they get to ride shotgun in the pickup with their masters to the hardware and feed stores, and they have more opportunities for mischief. They get to chase woodchucks, rabbits, and skunks. Not many urban dogs get to experience the offensive squirt from one of those black creatures with two white racing stripes down their back.

We have passed through several farm dogs on our homestead. The first two were simple Heinz 57 mixtures, but probably mostly Labrador. We got off to a poor start as our first ran off soon after we got it and was never seen again. The second lasted longer, but as I mentioned earlier, farm dogs like ours were free to roam, which, in this case, did not end well. I received a phone call from our neighbor from across the street, only to tell me that he just shot and killed our dog. He suspected that it was our dog who had raided his chicken coop the previous night. He had not witnessed the event and could not prove it, but he shot the dog he knew belonged to us. The act defies logic and compassion. I scooped the dog up and brought him home for a proper burial. I don't recall an apology being offered; we never spoke again.

The third dog was a keeper. A cousin contacted me to ask if I would be interested in a yellow lab pup. It was from a thoroughbred litter, but owners had no papers, and the dog could be had for free. I was going through a divorce at the time, and adopting one of man's best friends seemed like a good idea. I named her Tamara and raised her in our cellar. When she completed puppyhood, she became a barn dog. She had a horse stall all to herself with plenty of bedding hay. She got to be out every day, free to assist me with the day's work. She became exceptionally loyal, as most dogs do. She would follow me everywhere, no matter the task. On mowing days, she would run up and down orchard rows, shadowing the tractor on every circuit. Her tongue became long and pink. It looked like something a cartoon artist had drawn onto her jaws. Eventually, she would stop to rest and wait until I had finished the field.

Tamara was a retriever, and this trait became her specialty. Her bait started off with the proverbial stick and, for no sound reason, later became stones and small rocks. Tamara was relentless with this throw-and-fetch routine. As she aged, it became an addiction for her. If someone were to drive up to the farm, the driver would immediately have a rock deposited at their feet. Everyone took the cue and tossed the rock, and it didn't matter where you threw it. I made hundreds of attempts to throw her rock as far as I could and in places hard to get at just to slow the fetch cycle down. She hardly ever returned without a rock, and it was the same rock tossed. She would repeat the cycles until her tongue grew long, and then she was beat, at least for a little while.

There were times when I would tease Tamara with an "air" throw or "no rock in my hand" throw. She would routinely deposit a stone at my feet to let me know she was ready for a toss-and-fetch exercise. A stone would be dropped within twelve inches of my shoe, then she would take position ten feet away, poised on all fours, with every muscle in her body tensed, ears at attention, brown eyes fully open and focused on mine, mouth closed. I would bend down, pick up the rock, perform a major league pitcher wind-up, and unload nothing. By the time my arm reached its apex, Tamara was off on the hunt, scanning the horizon, expecting to see and then hear the rock come to earth. She quickly realized the rock had not left my hand and returned to her earlier position. I repeated all the actions I just described, and Tamara dashed off again. This time, she didn't sprint out as far and returned. I could do this two more times, and then she parked herself a couple feet away, cocked her head, and if she could speak, would have said, "What's up, Dad?"

Winter brought with it some new opportunities for Tamara and more teasing schemes for me. The ground was usually frozen and snow-covered. The change in conditions reduced Tamara's rock find success rate. Rocks thrown into a snow-covered field did create a serious challenge, but she still managed to find many of them. The ultimate tease was when I scooped up some snow and made a snowball. I would bend down and show her what appeared to be a white rock. She assumed her usual, ready-to-fetch position; I did my windup and released the frozen projectile. She did her best, making multiple zig-zag passes in the snow, but usually returned empty-mouthed, panting heavily, having given the futile search her best effort.

Tamara was in heaven on winter Saturday mornings. Those were the days I would do the cow slaughtering. This process has been common within clans or tribes and on farms for thousands of years. It is uncommon now as the USDA has put the kibosh on it. Tamara would participate by lapping up blood and sucking down strips of fat. It was particularly humorous to watch her carry off a hoof. With hoof in mouth, it looked as if she was trotting off with her hind legs off the ground. She would return from sequential trips with a cut and bleeding nose, having attempted to bury her find in the snow and ice to save it for later.

One spring day, I set out to spray the plum orchard down from the house and, at one point, looked up to see MaryEllen running from the direction of our house with arms flailing in the air. She was very animated, agitated, and obviously trying to get my attention. I drove over to her as quickly as I could, and as I opened the tractor cab door, she blurted out, "Tamara's been shot!" We had a neighbor (not the same neighbor who shot dog number two) to our north, about 200 feet beyond a common stone wall between us. There was a compound of a couple of houses with apartments and a separate single-family home. Tamara must have gone on a reconnaissance mission to their garbage can. MaryEllen told me she was sitting at the kitchen table reading the newspaper when there was one loud shot followed by Tamara's broken run from their side of the wall. She had been shot in the right front leg just below the elbow. We called the vet and sped over to their facility. Tamara and I rode over in the back of the pickup. This happened nearly thirty years ago, but the image remains crystal clear: I have my hand clamped around her leg to stop the bleeding. I talked to her for the entire trip, asking her to hold on.

The vet performed a great save, the leg healed, and Tamara went on to run another day. Upon return from the vet, I called the local police and reported the incident. Three hours passed with no response. I called again and upped the urgency in my voice. Many hours later, a squad car finally arrived. A young officer took down the details, but nothing became of it. We finally deduced

In These Veins

Tamara

that our neighbor's compound was owned by the town board member who sat on the police liaison committee. Lesson learned from that event: Should an incident like this ever occur again, call the DEC—Department of Environmental Conservation—instead of the police. It is illegal to shoot a firearm within 500 feet of a building. An incident like this falls under their jurisdiction, and calling them would likely yield better results.

Tamara lived on to have a great life. There were more dogs to come and go, but these pups lived in our house and were only out on the farm on a leash. In my opinion, dogs like my sweet Tamara lead a privileged life and, I suspect, are proud to be called a Farm Dog.

SEVENTEEN

It's Spring—
Let's Move the Pigs

*The annual process of getting young
piglets started on our farm was always entertaining.
What could possibly go wrong?*

Our early farm products included rabbits, beef, pork, and chicken. Each March, I got in touch with my farmer friend Howard to see when his litters of pigs were expected. He had several sows which produced multiple litters each year. We had purchased our farm from Howard and his two cousins. Howard was a unique individual. He preferred to live in another era. He was of a stocky build, wore a salty, bushy beard, and didn't drink, smoke, or curse. In his prime, he could hoist a forty-pound bale of hay onto a trailer bed with one hand. His pants belt was yellow baling twine. He cut hay and spread manure with a pair of mules. People who knew him would say, "It looks like you're living in the past." Howard would politely respond, "And that's the way I like it."

Howard and Omar Charlie

Back to the pork pickup. I was prepared to pick up the "porklets" when they were about a month old. I used our pickup truck for their short trip to our farm. Preparation for their arrival was always preceded by the annual mucking out of the barn. The beef cows had free winter access to a small stanchion area and a box stall, and they filled the area with five months' accumulation of cow poop and wasted hay. My friend Bob, who had also grown up in Montgomery, assisted me with the annual ritual. He seemed to enjoy the diversion from his engineering day job. We got caught up about events in our lives, asked about siblings, and shared who we had recently seen from our high school class. I think we were procrastinating; it was time to start tossing the scented wafers out the door into the fifty-year-old John Deere wooden manure spreader. Okay, okay, it wasn't made of only wood; the sides were sheet metal steel, the frame was steel, as well as the spinning tines at the rear. Actually, it was all steel except for the wooden deck, but I wanted it to sound like it was an antique, which it actually was. The radio was tuned to the local rock station, WPDH, playing "White Rabbit," being belted out by Grace Slick. After a few hours, the barn was clean and ready for the piglets.

The little pork chops were started on powdered milk and then moved to regular feed over the span of two months. By June, the days were warming, signaling the time to move them outside. I made the usual inspections of their summer quarters. Yes, it was called "the pigpen." I checked the pen for escape holes. Pigs are exceptionally good at moving earth with their hard-rimmed noses. If given the right opportunity, they can, over time, move literally tons of earth. With all escape routes blocked, I got the water working, and their summer home was ready.

The young pigs had been in the box stall since their arrival. Pigs grow fast, and each already weighed about thirty-five pounds. In any one year, we raised seven to ten of them. I prepared for the move up the hill to the pen. I stationed the pickup at the back barn door and then went to the house to put on my rattiest farm clothes. If you did not know this, pigs are one of the slinkiest creatures on the planet. Male goats share a similar distinction. I went to the stall and mentally prepared for the event. The pigs were happily rooting about the floor, seeking out any morsel missed from the morning feeding. As soon as I approached, they froze in their tracks and stood frozen until I said something. Then, they would race around in circles until, for whatever reason, they decided to stop and freeze again. I only mention this because they always did this, and I found it comical. It was like their version of the kids' game Freeze Tag.

Once I had my concentration focused, I entered the stall, and the games began. I eyed the first one, and it darted toward me, but it was too fast, and as he sliced between my legs, my arms grabbed nothing but air. The pigs zigged and zagged across the pen, kicking up pig poop in the process. They looked like greased, four-legged, brown leather footballs, which, when you think about it, is what their hide can become. I eventually captured one and hauled it to the truck. I repeated the process of lunging at each of the animated projectiles. Each time I made a capture, I essentially had to give it a bear hug to maintain the catch. You get the picture, as it wasn't long before I looked and smelled like one of them. I finished the process and headed to the house. I felt my wife's eyes on me; she smelled me before I even got close. There would be a designated wash load that afternoon!

EIGHTEEN

The Gasket

It is very helpful for a farmer to have a broad skill set. I thought my knowledge scope was robust and competent until I faced off with a gasket.

I DECIDED THAT THE FARM-RAISED MEAT BUSINESS WOULD BE a good fit for our new homestead. I could easily raise animals and simultaneously mold my IBM career. I knew fellow workers at IBM would buy my products. They were already putting in orders for eggs. My daughter Michele, ten years old at the time, and I were in the egg business. She would bravely enter the chicken coop at dawn and, with one eye on the rooster, collect and prep the eggs each day. I would take care of trucking and sales. We split the daily one-dozen egg sale of one dollar per dozen fifty-fifty.

The pork was one of our meat offerings. This was all me. No partnership here. I built a pen for our pigs, some 250 feet away from the house. Pigs don't necessarily smell good. The separation kept our house stink-free. Their drinking water was pumped from a hand-dug well located just south and west of the barn. We would also use the water to mist the pigs on hot days.

The well was likely dug in the early 1800s. It was fed from spring water, first flowing into a cast iron bathtub and the overflow passing into the well. The tub also served as a water source for all the larger livestock roaming the farm.

In summer, the recharge rate by the spring was a little weak. The well contents could be pumped down quickly. I had done some probing and deduced that the well bottom was filled with muck. The silty mud reduced the well's capacity to hold water, so I decided it had to go. I waited for the driest time of summer and pumped the well dry. With my son Doug's help, we began the dredge. We used a small steel bucket with a rope secured to the bail. I donned my fishing waders and descended with a bucket in hand down a small ladder to the bottom. The well was ten feet deep and about three-and-a-half feet across. This would be defined as a claustrophobic space. I was not happy being down there; the humidity was stifling. The rock-lined wall coated with cold green slim was inches from my face. Were there any snakes down here? Maybe this is what it might have felt like for a dungeon-jailed convict in medieval times. I filled the bucket with brown muck and then yelled to Doug so he could haul it to the top; he dumped out the stinky payload and sent the bucket back down to me. In a couple hours, we were done. We probably increased the well's volume by twenty-five percent.

Prior to this project, I had disconnected the shallow well pump perched on the well's wooden cover. Afterward, I reconnected the pump and flicked the switch. The water seemed to be moving through the piping as expected for a minute, followed by a faint screech, silence, and a tiny curl of smoke. A swear word was likely muttered. I thought the pump must have pulled in some sediment and seized up. I poked around the barn and found another pump. I disconnected the dead pump at the flange interface. The old flange gasket tore during the process. I had no matching gasket inventory but had some bulk stock. I carefully traced the flange

Me in well

profile onto the rubber, replicating its shape and mounting holes, made the cuts, and we were good to go.

I attached the homemade gasket, reassembled the flanges, and flicked the switch. The motor quietly purred, but there was no flow. I pondered the situation at length. Now, keep in mind that I am a person with considerable knowledge of mechanics. I have a degree in mechanical engineering and solve mechanical problems at IBM on a daily basis. I was familiar with fluid flow, vacuums, and pressure, but I couldn't, for the life of me, figure out why water wouldn't flow from this well. I carefully analyzed the sequence of things to no avail. It was frustrating.

I broke for lunch and went into the house. MaryEllen saw my furrowed face and asked what the matter was. I described what I had done step by step, and without missing a heartbeat, she asked, "Did you cut out the center of the gasket?" The problem had stumped my mechanical engineer's brain, yet MaryEllen, a former English teacher with a master's degree in Education of the Deaf, solved the problem in one breath. What the f*ck?!!

NINETEEN

Scorched Orchard

Farmers often start fires to dispose of tree trimmings and brush. The technical term for these fires is called a "controlled burn." This one was not.

IN THE EARLY NINETIES, I DECIDED WE COULD SELL MORE peaches, but there were not enough trees planted to produce more fruit. We needed more acreage for additional trees. At the top of our mountain farm, there was a long, overgrown field. It had last been a cornfield in the forties. It was now fully wooded with trees, each one twelve inches across and thirty feet tall. Many of the trees were engulfed by poison ivy and wild grape vines. Clearing the three-acre field was going to be a challenge. It was about this time that I met MaryEllen. The clearing of the field coincidently happened during our courtship. She was a teacher living in Maryland at the time. We attempted to alternate the five-hour drive, either to Maryland or New York, to spend the weekend together, but honestly, she came to New York a lot more often than I went to Maryland. MaryEllen arrived at the farm on Friday nights. As timing would have it, we spent Saturday cutting trees and brushes in preparation for the new peach orchard. The cut trees made great firewood, and there was a lot of it. We spent numerous Saturdays corralling the wood into piles and then hauling trailer loads down the mountain. The effort would be considered strenuous by most standards. Most of our clearing effort was being accomplished during upstate New York's winter months. Many of the Saturday clearing events were performed with the thermometer reading 20° Fahrenheit. Our fingers and toes were not very happy. It will likely go down in our memoirs as "testing MaryEllen," but that was not how I saw it then.

Once the firewood was moved, more work would follow. We had no specialized equipment at that time, so all the tree trimmings had to be moved by hand. We produced large piles scattered all about the new field. For a couple of Saturdays, the effort was focused on burning the brush.

My son, Doug, was a college student at the time, living at home to save money and putting in some hours on the farm to make money. During one of my weekend visits to Maryland, I assigned Doug to burn detail. Doug was not new at this, as we had disposed of many brush piles together, so I journeyed to Maryland with confidence.

The new peach orchard was not contiguous with the rest of the farm. It was surrounded on three sides by woods. The fourth side bordered an adjacent farm to the south, separated by a stone wall. From our barn, we accessed the new space via an existing orchard and then through some woods.

Having returned from Maryland and spent the work week at IBM, I headed up the mountain the following Saturday to finish burning. As I approached the crest of the mountain, my eyes picked up on some blackened skeletons of red cedar trees. I was looking at the wooded area preceding the new space. As I progressed closer, I noticed all the grass was blackened. The entire wood lot looked like the result of one of those western wildfires we hear about in the news too often these days. I peered to the north, and those woods looked the same. I finally got to the new peach site, and it, too, was completely scorched. The fire had long gone out. I continued my forensic efforts. In the final analysis, most of our hilltop had burned. By rights, the fire should have burned the entire Marlboro Mountain. Yet, for some magical reason, the fire didn't push through an opening in the stonewall to advance to the neighbor's eighty-acre field of grass. Perhaps there was not enough tinder for the flames to ignite, or maybe the wind subsided.

I confronted Doug when he returned from college that night. He knew nothing about the wildfire. He did admit he should have tended the fire a little longer before heading out for a night with his friends.

He now has the eternal nickname of SCORCH.

TWENTY

Wildlife, Livestock, and "He Just Served Her"

From turtles in my youth to beef cattle, pigs, rabbits, and chickens later, here are some details about how my professional farming career got started and some unique and often comical events that occurred in those early farming days.

STARTING A FARM FROM SCRATCH CAN BE A fINANCIALLY CHALlenging endeavor. The list of equipment needed to tackle farm tasks seems to have no end. One approach to securing capital could be taking out a bank loan if you could find a willing lender. Another approach could be a "buy as you go" strategy, using any extra money you could glean from your day job paycheck. We chose the latter tactic, and I suspect many people who want to be farmers have chosen the same path as we did. Our farm was started in 1979.

Our farm was initially named Stoneside Farm after the many stone walls that line the border and dissect the farm into separate fields. When we went into farming full-time, we changed the name to Glorie Farms; it's the family surname, and it seemed to be the right thing to do. I later found out that our place had been called Sunnyside in the past. The farm sits on the east side of the Marlboro Mountains and is illuminated immediately when the sun rises.

Raising livestock was a fairly easy way to both farm and hold down a full-time job. I did have some previous experience raising rabbits and then with cattle at my job at the Hoeffner farm. I even had experience raising turtles.

For some reason, which I cannot explain, at the age of about ten, I decided to gather up some wild turtles. I built a wooden pen that featured a micro pond (metal basin), a barn (inverted wooden box), some leaves and grass for nesting, and places for the turtles to hide. I'm sure capturing and confining the little creatures was illegal, but I didn't know this, and the turtle police never showed up.

In the spring of this particular year, I gathered up some spotted turtles, painted turtles, and wood turtles. I must have gotten the gender mix right, as they actually laid fertile eggs. The eggs hatched, and now I had a turtle farm. Have you ever wondered how turtles mate? I didn't think so, but I did when I was writing this book. It turns out they do it just like dogs, cats, and rabbits. It must be sort of like watching two rocks mate.

Now that I was armed with this vast livestock experience, we went into the beef business. Inevitably, while raising livestock, there will be a need to call a veterinarian. One day, we observed one of our Angus heifers bumping into things as she moved about the yard. This continued for a couple of days, so we decided to call the vet. He arrived, did the usual check for vitals, and found nothing unusual. The next thing I knew, he was making swatting motions with his hand toward the cow's face. The cow never blinked or moved away. It turned out our heifer couldn't see; the likely reason was lead poisoning. One of the symptoms of lead poisoning is blindness. The vet suspected our girl picked it up somewhere on the farm. We did a short stroll around the barnyard and its perimeter, and in short order, we found the source. I had parked our corn picker in a pasture area our cows accessed daily. I had applied used motor oil as a chain lubricant on the picker. This was a time when leaded gasoline was still being used. The oil picked up lead from the engine's combustion of gasoline. The cow must have licked and ingested a small amount of the toxic oil. I moved the corn picker out of the pasture, and sometime later, the cow's sight returned on its own.

Cows never seem to be content to stay where they're supposed to be. Most of our containment was done via an electric fence, which is cost-effective but not reliable. MaryEllen's hearing is much better than mine. One night, as we prepared to sleep, MaryEllen heard something walking in the yard right outside the bedroom window above our heads. She whispered, "Did you hear that?" Having heard nothing, I said in a normal voice, "Hear what?" She quickly got out of bed and squinted into the darkness outside. Seeing nothing out of the one window, she moved to look out another. There, she thought she saw the outline of a large animal, so she said, "I think there's a cow in the backyard." Thinking this was absurd, I said, "No, there isn't. Come back to bed." She stayed where she was and insisted, "I think there's a cow out there!" I shook my head and said, "Stop it. Just come back to bed." Right about then, there was a loud "MOO!!!" I jumped out of bed, looked into the backyard, and then back to MaryEllen and said, "There's a cow in the backyard!" She said, "That's what I said!" We both dissolved in laughter. We both got up and got dressed, then we headed outside with flashlights in hand and coaxed the cow back into the pasture through the same break in the fence through which it had made its midnight escape. A quick mend was made, and we went back to bed.

Cows tend to not like being confined, especially when it's not their choice. On this day, we needed to isolate a Hereford steer. We ushered him into our box stall. The stall was twelve feet square with two walls constructed of concrete floor to ceiling. Another wall was made of wood with steel bars and a door. The fourth side was just wood four feet high. MaryEllen was monitoring as I had to leave the barn for a moment.

I had not been gone more than thirty seconds when I heard MaryEllen screaming for me. I scrambled back to find a highly frightened wife attempting to push 1,600 pounds of beef off the wall and back into the stall. Needless to say, the future needs to contain our herd would be done with greater scrutiny.

Many wild animals found their way onto the farm from time to time. Most of them would have descriptions like a cute rabbit, a stinky skunk, or a majestic deer. But what about snakes? In our area, one of the dominant snakes is the black racer. We usually just refer to them as black snakes. Invariably, I got an annual summer call from the wife frantically summoning my snake wrestling skills to the house. Black snakes love to seek out bird eggs, even if they are in birdhouses. By the time I arrived, all I would see was the snake's tail protruding from the birdhouse. After several minutes of tugging, the snake was removed and returned to the wild.

There was a snake event that got my attention in the early days of Stoneside Farm. I arrived at our rabbitry one morning to find a black snake inside one of the cages. A doe had recently birthed a litter. The cage was constructed of one-inch chicken wire walls. The snake had been able to pass into the cage through the wire wall but not back out, as he had a baby rabbit inside him. His diameter was now two inches around. This snake was not returned to the wild.

Soon after I lost my job at IBM, we decided to expand our farming operation and make a go of it full-time. We were in the tree fruit business, and as such, it took years to pick the first fruit. Growing tree fruit is quite different from raising cattle or pigs or even vegetables, for that matter. Vegetables can be harvested in less than six months, pigs about the same, and beef cattle in eighteen to twenty months. Pears need nine years, peaches four years, and apples three to six years, depending on what rootstock is used. We were in a hurry to get some income flowing, so we experimented with some shortcuts. One of them was raising roasting chickens. This project only took a few months rather than years until harvest. I purchased seventy-five chicklets, and off we went. A few months passed, and we were ready to slaughter. I asked my friend Hank, an avid hunter and fisherman, to assist. I did the slaughtering and Hank the dunking. The chicken murders were straightforward, as I simply cut off their heads. My sister, Jeanne, being a professional welder, had fabricated a gas-fired "chicken cooker." Once dead, the chicken body must be dunked into boiling water to enable plucking of the feathers. After the first few, we developed a rhythm, but it still took several hours until finally, all seventy-five chickens were processed. The dominant color in the scene was red. The ground, the barn walls, Hank, and I were covered in blood. I soon decided the chicken business was not for me. It was simply too much effort and too little profit.

Our Stoneside Farm also boasted of a pork business. I would buy some piglets and raise them to finished weight. I would arrange with the grower to sell them to me castrated if there were males in the litter. Removing the males' testicles made all the difference in the meat's flavor. One year, my farmer friend Howard, also a supplier of our piglets, stopped by to see how I was doing. I was still a newbie then, and he had forty years of experience. We were at the pigpen observing my drove—short for a group of pigs—when Howard pointed toward a couple of pigs and casually remarked, "He just served her." It's a phrase I had not heard before and never heard again, and I found the phrase humorous, so much so that I included it in the title of this chapter. But clearly, it was part of Howard's farm vocabulary. One of the pigs must have benefited from a castration malfunction and was having an enjoyable experience. We kept a keen eye on the females of the drove to see if they became pregnant, but none did. There must have been some other malfunction with our single-balled boar.

The pork production season always passed by quickly, and soon it was time to load the pigs for market. It had become my least desired task of the year. Like most livestock, pigs don't like to be put into small places.

I enlisted Howard's assistance for this task since he had a small cattle truck. He backed the truck over to the pen, and we hastily constructed a temporary loading chute. I had cut off the pigs' feed a day earlier. I placed feed on the ramp and inside the truck to entice them in. We were almost ready to load. The scene was set. By scene, I mean picture the pen, if you will. It is a PIG pen. Pigs are not known to be tidy creatures. They had been in their pen for several months and had no housekeeping skills. I took a long, slow, deep breath, gave the signal, and the circus commenced with pigs flying in every direction. It reminded me of the Johnny Cash song "My Name is Sue." There is a line that contains the phrase "in the mud and the blood and the beer." There was no beer at this point, but there was lots of mud and a little blood, probably most of which was mine.

The first few porkers loaded without an issue, and then the scene changed. Howard stayed in the back of the truck securing a makeshift gate to keep the loaded porkers in the truck. The remainder of the pig pack refused to cooperate. I needed to push each remaining screeching pork chop up the ramp. The event eventually concluded, and off they went to market.

Our livestock days did come to an end, but there are still days when I entertain the thought of having a few cows. Even now, on our retirement farm, I turn to MaryEllen from time to time and say, "We should get some cows." Every time, her answer is the same, a slow shake of the head and a simple yet firm "No."

TWENTY-ONE

The Cows Are Out Again

Confining domestic cattle in fields and pastures has challenged farmers for centuries. Cows are always breaching their fences no matter what they are made of. This was no different for our farm.

AT THE BEGINNING OF OUR QUEST TO BE FARMERS, ONE OF our main products was freezer beef. The cycle began with the arrival of day-old calves in November. I bottle-fed these fragile bovines morning and evening, before and after my day job. They were always delighted to see me, playfully bumping my leg with their noses, wishfully thinking that mom's udder was nearby with a warm teat full of milk. Some evenings, I was assisted by my children, Doug and Michele; we were the calves' surrogate mothers for several weeks. Eventually, I got them onto solid food, which sped up the feeding routine. Spring would soon arrive, with warm temperatures nudging the pasture to green up once again. The greening of the grass was the signal to turn the now 200-pound calves out to pasture.

Our fencing primarily consisted of a single strand of electrified

Michele and Doug nursing calves

steel wire. I will admit that the wire was not easy to see. Maybe I was hoping the little fellas shared the highly acclaimed vision of birds. After all, there must have been some species of flying cows 10,000 years ago.

Turning the cows out to pasture became a spring ritual. They only knew the four walls of their box stall for the last five months. They didn't know what the sun, sky, and space were all about. And they clearly had no respect for electricity and a wimpy piece of wire.

I would summon my first wife, Josie, and kids and arrange them strategically outside of the fence. The concept was to allow the young steers to approach the fence slowly, test the wire with their nose, receive their initial shock, and be immediately trained for the season.

The plan fell apart in short order, as it always has. With the family at their stations, I turned the herd loose, and the games began. They immediately embraced their freedom, bucking up and down, kicking up their hooves, and bolting toward the open space. The family cowhands waved their arms, yelling strange calls to no avail. The young, frisky steers sailed through the electrified wire too quickly to know where the shock came from. Once they settled down a bit, we got them inside the fence. They often repeated this stunt one more time but eventually gained respect for that nagging jolt.

We went through this annual cycle beginning in 1979 and continuing into the '90s. The demand for freezer beef slowed as people's fear of high cholesterol grew, so they tried to reduce their dependence on filet mignon and rump roasts. This was okay as we had been planting more trees and vines each year, which reduced the amount of available pasture. We started purchasing some hay in summer, which nipped away at our profit. There really wasn't much margin anyway. I got more satisfaction from watching the cows chewing their cud than watching the checkbook. Over time, as we shrunk pasture acreage, the cows were tempted to reach a little beyond the wire to try to get a couple more mouthfuls of grass. If I was not vigilant with the fence maintenance, grass or brush could grow into the wire and easily short it out, rendering the wire shockless. The cattle found these opportunities from time to time and pushed under or through the wire. We could easily nudge them back. The steers were generally low-key and gentle.

There was an escape event—not precipitated by the cows' hunger—in the winter of 1987. My daughter, Michele, a teenager at the time, hosted an outdoor going away party for her best friend, Laura. Michele had invited thirty of her classmates to the farm to celebrate Laura's departure. Practicing her usual, conscientious behavior, Michele suggested that we should confine the cows to their wood-lined corral for the evening. I agreed, and with the cows safely secured behind a wood fence and gates, I retired to the house to give the kids some privacy. Soon, the kids started arriving, and the party commenced. Sometime later, the bon fire was blazing, flames leaping ten feet, boom boxes amped up, kids dancing to the beat. The cows, on the other hand, had not witnessed sights and sounds like this before. They soon became confused and agitated, broke down the metal gate, and stampeded the young crowd. Adrenalin flooded the kids' bodies, and they quickly scattered. One of the girls slid down an embankment, fracturing her leg. Many of the rest of the kids pushed through the night hidden electric fence wire. They received a little shock, but no lasting injuries occurred. I am sure this image is etched into Michele's memory forever!

During the next year, the cows' propensity to escape began to increase. One gorgeous fall day, we dressed in formal clothing, got in the car, and headed out to an afternoon wedding. Town watershed property bordered us to the south. As we reached the bottom of the driveway and turned south onto the town road, MaryEllen peered across the stonewall and then leaned toward me. She pointed into the woods and asked, "Whose cows are those?" I replied, "They're ours!" We headed back to the house and changed into our farming uniforms. We missed the church ceremony and half the reception. This marked the beginning of the end of cows for us. As winter progressed, their escapades off the farm continued. I was able to lure them back on these occasions by smacking two feed buckets together, and in short order, they would show up at the barn to fill their bellies.

On one mid-winter day, however, the bucket trick elicited no response. I tried several iterations to no avail; the cows did not come home. The next morning, I set out on the four-wheeler. It had snowed overnight, which made the tracking process easier. The cows had first gone west to the top of the farm, then north onto a neighboring abandoned farm to an old logging road about a half mile from our barn. The logging road, really a path, was flanked by a mountain on the east and a swamp to the west. I tracked their movement, now heading south, and at one point, I looked up, and there they were. My little herd numbered five at this stage, but there were only four in sight. They were simply standing there and had been for some time, telling from several pies of poop. I looked about and found the fifth cow. It had walked out onto the swamp ice and had fallen through. The ice lip, in concert with the swamp muck, locked him in. He was going nowhere, and the other cows simply would not leave their comrade. The trapped cow looked lethargic, which made sense since it had been submerged in thirty-two-degree water for likely half a day.

I was not going to be able to figure out how this happened, but a neighbor was out riding his horse on the wood road, traveling north toward me and the cow debacle. As luck would have it, he had a rope, and he offered to help. He positioned his horse at the swamp edge, and we tied the rope to the cow. He then urged his horse forward to pull the cow out, but there was too much resistance between the ice rim, mud, and weight of the cow. After all, we had but one horsepower to work with. We had to give up on this rescue approach. I thanked the neighbor for his effort and headed back down to the house.

I left a note for MaryEllen on the kitchen table and placed her walkie-talkie on the note. Cell phones were not yet available. The note said, "Cows are out again. Please call me, I am going to need your help." I was expecting her home at about 3:00. I took my walkie-talkie, a rope, and the John Deere tractor. I was now loaded with forty-seven horsepower. I got back to the site where the boys were still watching over their herdmate. The trapped cow was still with us, but I was certain he was tiring and fading. I positioned the Deere on the edge of the swamp and tied the rope onto the draw bar. I carefully walked the other end across the ice, thankful it supported my weight, and placed it around the steer's neck. It was the only feature of the cow I had access to. I returned to the tractor. At this juncture, I was either going to kill this cow while trying to save it, or I would free it from its soon-to-be death. I eased the throttle up, and the tractor slowly moved away from the swamp. The cold, submerged body started to move with rope tensioning. Fortunately, the ice began to break as the rope pressured through it, functioning like a ship's ice breaker. A few hopeful moments passed, and I got our boy to solid ground. I quickly removed the rope. The cow was cold and quite weak. I gave him a little time to acclimate, but I really needed to get him on his feet, back to the barn, warmed up, and fed. I nudged his rump with a few shoe taps. He finally stood up, wobbly and shivering. I believe I heard some moo cheers across the way.

I ushered our survivor over to his pack. They were all smiling ear to ear, and I realize it's difficult to tell when a cow is smiling but trust me, they were smiling. They all ambled over to him and licked off the water and mud. Even under normal circumstances, cows are good at this licking routine. At this point, I needed to shuffle the little herd back to familiar ground. The cows didn't know where they were or what direction to move in. They must take cues from me. As I approached them, they moved away, and we were off to a good start. Just then, I heard MaryEllen's voice on the walkie-talkie. To my relief, she was headed up the mountain. Cows are much easier to move with two people. MaryEllen soon found us, and the round-up went smoother. We finally got out of the woods and back to familiar ground. The cows perked up and quickened their pace. They managed to exit the main farm road several times through openings in the stone wall into pasture or fruit orchards, but we managed to corral them back to the road without much difficulty. They soon caught up on a few missed meals.

This was the last herd we raised on the farm. From here on, we were strictly a fruit farm! I do miss having the cattle on our

Doug Jr. and me with dressed steer

farm, but they simply did not produce enough profit. MaryEllen and I will visit some of our cattle-raising friends on occasion to get our cow "fix." We recently visited Barbera Masterson and her sister Lynn Faurie of B & L 4E Farms nearby to admire their herd. Barbera is a talented artist, and while we were there, I purchased one of her original paintings of their white-faced Herefords. It hangs on the wall just to the left of my keyboard, so all I need to do is turn my head to see cattle anytime I wish.

TWENTY-TWO

Row Not Straight

Tree fruit farmers take a lot of pride in having an orderly matrix of trees in any one orchard. The rows simply must be straight!

People are sometimes classified as Type A or perhaps Type B. I would say my wife, MaryEllen, is a Type A+. She tries very hard to do tasks to perfection, though I have spent the past thirty-two years trying to get her to become more of an A-. I haven't had much success. I, too, could be classified as a Type A person; however, I continuously strive to become a B, to be able to accept a result somewhere short of perfection. It is one of my life's goals.

We planted many trees during our tenure on the farm. It was essentially a tree fruit farm with apples, pears, peaches, plums, and some quince trees. We also grew about eight acres of wine grapes. Till about 1995, we were in a tree planting mode. There was a section of land on the east side of our driveway that was vacant and begging to have something planted on it, so I ordered enough apple trees to fill the space. It was a fairly small area and would only support about thirty trees, but it featured a desirable, sloping, easterly exposure. The trees arrived quite early, in the first part of April. With my standard eighteen-inch diameter auger mounted on the back of my tractor, I attempted to drill holes in the earth to plant the trees in, but I didn't have much success because it was a very rocky area with shaley veins close to the surface. The rows were to be fifteen feet apart, and it seemed as though every row was directly in line with a vein of shale just below the earth. It was very frustrating; the auger wouldn't drill into the rock. Normally, it would take just sixty seconds to produce a planting hole. I finally resorted to using a pick—or pickaxe—followed by a handheld hammer pounding on a steel driver to get down deep enough and remove the rock from the holes. You may now be thinking, *Why expend the extra effort, and how does an apple tree survive in a rock hole?* I am not advocating planting your next orchard on a granite slab, but my situation featured loosely bound, nearly vertical layers of shale. The fact is that fruit trees like to grow in this kind of rock. The tree's roots pierce fissures in the rock, seeking moisture and nutrients.

So, the pace of producing the tree holes had gone from one minute each with the auger to nearly an hour with the hammer and the steel chisel. The workday quickly passed, and there were still fifteen more holes to make. The situation was compounded by an uncertain overnight forecast featuring an approaching low-pressure system with temperatures of about thirty-two degrees. Would the skies drop rain, ice, or the white stuff? The mystery of the overnight weather was resolved by sunrise. The earth was now blanketed with ten inches of heavy snow. So, this was where my A-ness tendencies came back to life. I would not be defeated! I ended up shoveling out the snow from each of the remaining holes and then proceeded to go back with my hammer and my chisel and make each hole just big enough to plant a tree. All the trees were successfully planted, and I thought I was done. However, it so happens that my customary place at the dinner table had a view looking down at this recent planting. My chair position lined up directly with the center row, and I could plainly see that the first tree wasn't in line with the other nine trees. I couldn't take it, so the next day, I got my shovel, dug up the errant tree, and moved it over in line with the other nine trees, and then I was happy. So you see, even if you want to be a B, sometimes it's a struggle.

THIRTY-THREE

Ten Thousand Trees

The art of trimming trees and vines, starting with chaos and ending with artwork.

As you read this chapter, you are going to ask yourself, *Where did its name come from?* And that's a fair question. By 1998, our farm contained a combined total of ten thousand plants, mostly vines, and the remainder, trees. I simply liked the sound of "Ten Thousand Trees."

Every tree and vine on our farm got trimmed every year. It was a big deal. It consumes many man-hours, but the trimming process maintains the shape of the plant and promotes new growth. The task is performed during the dormant season while the plant is asleep, essentially before it starts its spring phenological cycle. Much of it is done in winter. Some winters yielded efficient working conditions, and some not so much. Trimming trees with eighteen inches of snow on the ground at ten degrees Fahrenheit with a twelve-mile-an-hour north wind is not efficient. My fingers were never happy with these conditions. I have very large hands, size 2XX, and to this day, I find it challenging to buy a pair of gloves that fit well and keep my hands warm. The process of trimming also included accessing the orchard or vineyard, so any meaningful snowfall meant not only plowing the driveway and yard but also the farm roads and head rows of orchards and vineyards.

As I mentioned, finding ideal trimming days was often elusive. Days with crusty knee-high snow and a slight thaw are okay but fatiguing. The cold early morning hours worked out fine, but as the sun warmed the air, the ice crust would no longer reliably support my weight, so with every two or three steps, I would be jarred to the frozen earth, never knowing which step would take me there.

I trimmed trees for thirty-eight years on our original farm. There are, however, also 600 apple trees on our retirement farm. I just returned from trimming a row before I set words to this paragraph. These mature trees, some reaching twenty feet tall, have not seen a pruning shear in five years. I am attempting to rejuvenate these trees because there is nothing uglier to my eyes than an abandoned apple orchard. I love trimming trees and vines! It brings out the little artistic creativity I have.

I do not have any classic art skills. I can't paint or play the guitar, and I can barely hold a tune. I am, however, skilled with stone masonry, and I'm a master vine trimmer.

For me, every tangled grapevine is a fresh canvas. My hand shears are my brush. I visualize what the final fruiting vine cordons could look like and start nipping away at the web of unruly canes. Unfortunately, there are very few color options to work with. Basically, I have a brown vine backed with white (snow) or more brown (earth) or blue (sky). But I am outdoors in the fresh air, feeling a cool breeze on my face, tracking the sun as the day's hours tick by, noting the passage of clouds with their ever-changing shapes, listening to eclectic music via my headset, and solving life's puzzles as I trim. My mind is free to go wherever it chooses.

Each snap of my shears gets me closer to my masterpiece. In ten minutes, I am done, and I move on to my next work of art; after all, half of my genes trace back to Holland, and wasn't Van Gogh Dutch?

TWENTY-FOUR

Stand Back from The Window

Weather events often control the outcome of a farming season. A hailstorm is one of those events

HAILSTORMS ARE ONE OF THE MOST TRAUMATIC AND DESTRUCtive events Mother Nature can throw at a farmer. The frozen pellets nearly always leave their mark on the surface of the fruit. Unfortunately, consumers classically won't buy fruit with any dings or dimples. I think they see cartoon images in their mind with a worm poking its head from an apple, so any scarred fruit must have a worm in it. Unfortunately, hail-marked fruit takes the apple box price from $20 to $4 literally in a few minutes. Hail events occur all over the world, and there is little one can do to protect from them.

I need to lead off this segment with some farm life task sequencing so you can more fully appreciate the effect of a hail event. I'll use apples as an example, but it applies to all tree fruit. In my mind, an apple farm cycle starts with the annual trimming or pruning of the tree. Each tree is thinned of some of its branches and shaped to invigorate the tree and permit light and air penetration. The task often consumes most of the winter season. As spring nears, the trimmings that litter the orchard floor are physically raked to the row centers, the area between two adjacent rows of apple trees, sometimes called the "tractor row." This effort results in a continuous mound of brush filling the tractor row, rendering it impassable. Most farms, including ours, purchase a brush-chopping implement that attaches to the rear of a tractor. This is a very heavy device containing many whirling hammers covered by a steel canopy. I would connect my chopper to my most powerful tractor and then drive it over the row of brush, traveling at one mile per hour with the tractor throttle set at maximum RPM. It's an efficient process to eliminate the debris and incorporate fresh organic matter back into the soil.

Spring is also a time when many farms apply pre-emergent weed control. Fertilizer and lime are applied. Each pass or task adds to the cost of producing a box of fruit. Crop protectants are applied as needed. Remember our scary worm friend. American consumers are not fond of tiny fruit, so the trees are often thinned of excess fruit by hand to allow the remaining fruit to grow large. And the costs continue to add up. The orchards are mowed and, in droughty years, irrigated. Fences are erected to keep the deer out. August is approaching, and we likely have invested $12 per box so far. More costs will be incurred as the season progresses. $#*&@Z, (that's the sound I hear as the mechanical adding machine adds up production costs).

One June, we were celebrating a belated birthday party for me in the lower level of our barn. My birthday is March 3, but we had found that attempting to have a party before the calendar says spring was just too risky. If precipitation was expected and the thermometer was showing 32°, our family and friends were not likely to venture out to our mountain farm. It was an idyllic early Sunday afternoon, featuring bright sun and light breezes. I had spruced up space in the barn, removing cobwebs, barn swallow

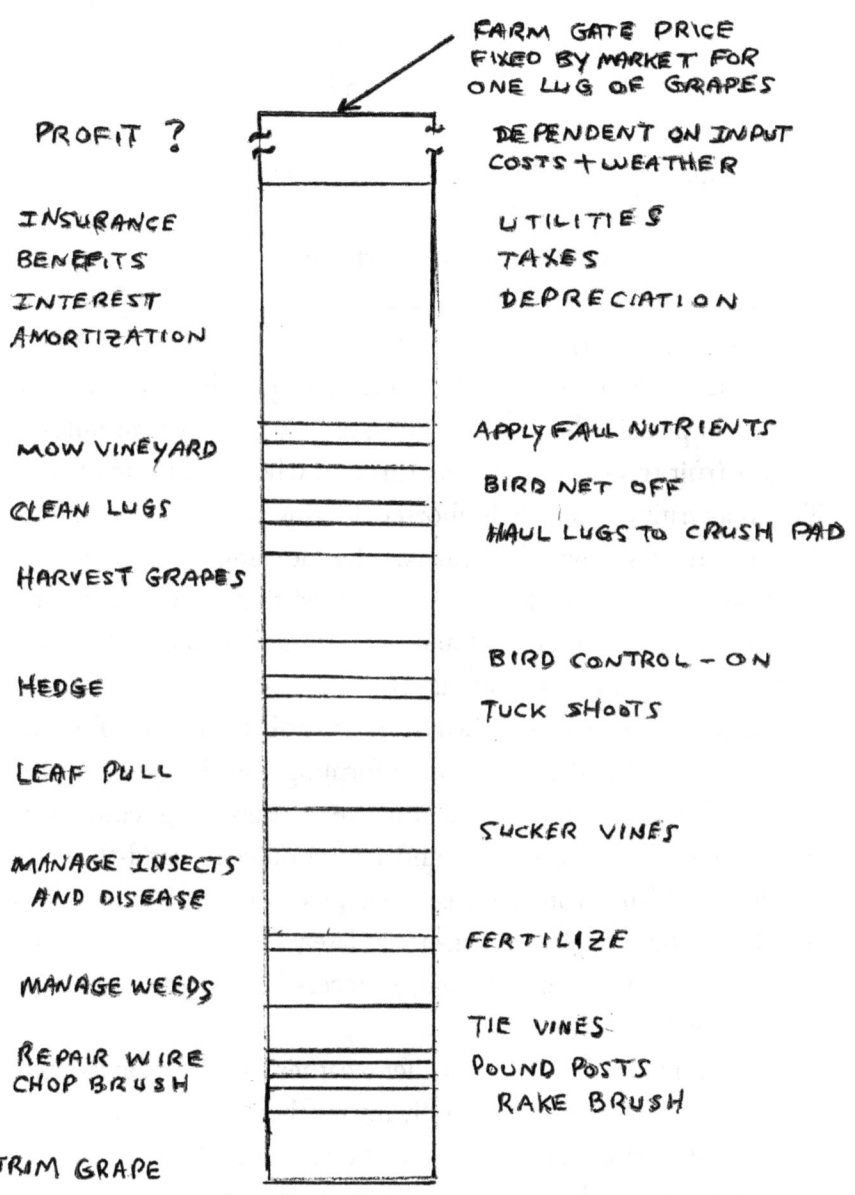

Profit Analysis Chart

nests, and mouse traps. Multicolored, non-matching chairs were spaced about the room. Our guests arrived, and we shared stories, wine, and food. My farmer friends bitched about the unusual spring like they always do. The party had not quite gone its natural duration when we noticed a change in the weather. The wind was picking up, bringing with it dark, low, mean-looking clouds. We couldn't do a quick check on our smartphones; they didn't exist yet. A severe thunderstorm was clearly on its way, and our guests decided to beat it out of there and get home before it arrived. Wind-driven rain arrived within twenty minutes of the last guest's departure. The rain came down in sheets, quickly followed by a barrage of pea-sized hail. The hail lasted for just three minutes.

Our fruit trees had just gone through what we call "fruit set." The weak fruit had naturally aborted, leaving the remainder of the crop to progress toward maturity. The morning after the hail, I went out to assess the damage and decided that thirty percent of the fruit was dimpled or cut and had no market value. My usual enthusiasm for the year had just taken a major hit. We now had one-third less fruit to sell; would there still be a profit for the year? It would be like your boss informing you that you will be taking a thirty percent pay cut. However, the growing season was still young, so the farm crew and I methodically hand-thinned the damaged fruit from the trees, one piece of fruit and one tree at a time. Three hundred man-hours later, the fruit looked good again. My optimism was restored; a successful year was now again in my sights!

Two months passed, and another weather event was on its way. On August 10, 1995, coincidentally my mother-in-law's seventieth birthday, at 2:00 a.m., I was awakened by the sound of heavy wind and booming thunder. I woke my deep-sleeping wife and told her, "There's a storm coming. It's going to be bad." We both got up and scurried to the living room as the wind was ferociously blowing from the west at our house. We lost power almost immediately.

There was lots of thunder accompanied by a Fourth of July display of lightning. And then Mother Nature added hail to the mix. It started with small pellets but quickly ramped up in size and density. Before long, quarter-size hail was smacking the windows and the glass French doors. Leaf fragments were splattered onto the glass. MaryEllen and I moved back from the window because we feared the glass was going to break.

The hail finally stopped after a ten-minute barrage, and the storm passed. I knew it was bad. I was unable to contain my anxiety about the possible damage, so I grabbed a flashlight and nervously walked out to the orchard just below the house to do an inspection. As I got closer, I thought, *Here we go again. As if one storm wasn't bad enough! All of the time, energy, and money spent thinning the trees back to good fruit just went out the window.* Hail stone strikes on an apple's surface take about twelve hours to really express themselves, but in this case, it was easy to see the effect as the apples were full of star-shaped cuts from the impacts. Under my feet, the earth was nearly white with three-quarter-inch frozen disks. I felt like I just stepped into a boxing ring and received one whopper punch to my gut. I brought several apples into the house. I showed them to MaryEllen via flashlight, and we sat on the living room couch in the dark for quite some time in silence, just completely stunned. Neither of us said it, but we both knew that all the farm profit potential that had existed just hours before when we went to bed had been destroyed. Feeling powerless, we returned to bed, but neither of us slept, and through the rest of the night, we would occasionally hear the snap of a tree, a branch finally breaking under its own weight after having been damaged in the storm.

The next morning, I set out to do a complete appraisal of the damage moving from orchard to orchard. It was worse than I could have imagined. I counted up to twenty-five hail hits per peach fruit. Twenty-five!! The hail was so intense that even peach tree bark was cut, mostly on the west side, as that's the direction the storm came from. These cut wounds would be a visible reminder for several years to come. I moved through the apple blocks, then to the Bosc pears, all displaying the same carnage. The apples were insured, so we would get back some of the money expended thus far for labor and materials. The other fruit was not. The pears would go to cider once they reached maturity. As for the peaches, much of the fruit had been knocked to the ground by the wind. The remaining damaged fruit would need to be removed due to disease pressure from a fungal pathogen, Monilinia fructicola, commonly called "brown rot." Shaking the tree could speed up the process, but if that didn't work, each remaining peach would need to be plucked from its branch. If the rot-infected peach fruit was left on the tree, the disease could migrate to the tree branches and cause tree death. At this point, I was asking my brain to come up with some sort of salvage concept. Surprisingly, there was a small amount of peach fruit—although mighty ugly—that was still sound, perhaps having been offered protection by branches and leaves. People tend to like a bargain. So, I invented the term "Touched by Nature" and marketed the dinged-up fruit at half price. This way, I was able to salvage at least some of our remaining peach crop, perhaps fifteen percent. We have used this technique numerous times over the years. It wouldn't be the last time Mother Nature called.

Grapes fared a little better. It didn't matter that the berries were pocked up. These were wine grapes and would simply be headed to the crusher at harvest. The crop condition was a little better on the east side of the vine as the clusters were afforded some protection from the vines' leaves and clusters on the west side of the vine.

There were to be more hail events in the years to come, but 1995 would go down as our most memorable. All bills and employees were paid. As is the case with many small farms, owners do not take a set salary. Whatever is left over at year-end is the owner's salary. I did the math for this year and concluded that I lost three dollars for every hour I worked. MaryEllen's employment off the farm saved us.

Hail events are very sporadic and unpredictable during any one day. They usually trace a narrow path, and in our area, they move from west to east. We could be experiencing an event, but our neighbor, just 1,000 feet to the south, may only feel a few or no pellets. Radar models continuously improve. Summer forecasts often include a chance for hail. These forecasts pique our interest, but it is when we pull the radar screen up on our phones that we really pay attention. I have learned over time that when a storm is headed in our direction and it has crisp storm lines and displays magenta color pigments, the likelihood of hail goes way up. These are high-anxiety days. I hear my mind repeating, *Will this be the day we lose our crop*? I know that there is nothing that can be done from a practical perspective to protect our diverse crop planting. When the hail does fall, you would really be better off not being near me. The loud expletives and enraged dancing might be too much to bear.

TWENTY-FIVE

Belted Bartletts

Fruit can, at times, be blemished by a weather event. Consumers are not likely to buy a piece of scarred fruit, but a farmer might salvage a crop with some assistance from a creative marketing tactic.

WEATHER CONTROLS NINETY-fiVE PERCENT OF ANY ONE YEAR'S farm profitability. Classically, if the weather is good, there will be a profit. The tree fruit business in New York State is temperature sensitive. It has more to do with cold than warmth. When we experience winter temps of negative twelve degrees or lower, there will be no peaches. Apples and pears are more tolerant and can squeak through negative twenty to thirty degrees Fahrenheit. The flower buds simply die at those levels. The buds do not regenerate, so we wait twelve months for the next potential crop.

Spring is another critical period. If we experience temps of seventy degrees in early March, this classically means trouble. High temps in early spring can advance the trees' phenology too quickly. Normally, apple trees bloom during the first week of May. Once a fruit bud is at or near the flowering phase, it is highly sensitive to cold. By cold, I mean temps below thirty-two degrees. In the mornings, when the thermometer is near 32°, we will hear the hum of wind machines in the valley below. Some farmers hire helicopters. On cold, still mornings, it may be twenty-six to thirty-two degrees at ground level but thirty-five degrees just thirty feet up. The wind machines and copter blades can mix these two air masses together and neutralize the temps to a benign level of thirty-two degrees. At thirty-two degrees, the fruit is safe.

Not all farms can afford these fan devices, so many farms lose their year's fruit production or, worse yet, experience partially damaged fruit. Complete losses are better for insurance claims.

So, what do you do with damaged fruit? Usually, it is used to produce some kind of cider or wine product. In the case of apples, a box of extra fancy Galas would fetch $20, but as cider quality, only $4. With pears, the scenario is similar.

During my farming career, I have tried to find a positive solution to turn around a troubling situation. Some twenty years ago, we experienced frost during the pear bloom. That year, the Bartlett pears emerged from their blossom, dressed with a brown frost ring around the circumference of their belly. It looked like the pears were headed for the cider mill. But then, a thought occurred to me. What if I were to market the fruit differently? The ring was merely a surface blemish. The pears tasted the same with or without the ring. So, I came up with the fanciful name of "Belted Bartletts" and sold all of them at a premium.

More marketing marvels were to follow. From 2004 to 2020, MaryEllen and I owned Glorie Farm Winery. We produced a spectrum of wines. In one particular year, we produced an apple wine and a pear wine. Neither of the wines produced robust sales, so what to do? How could we spark an increase in sales? I remembered my Belted Bartletts! We did a little experimentation, or as we would say in the wine business, "bench trials," and reinvented these two wines. We ended up disgorging the remaining cases of apple and pear wine, blended them together, and added a dash of sweetness and cinnamon. We named it after our mischievous chocolate Labrador, Sullivan, and we released it a second time as Sully's Cinful Pearple. It was so successful we were destined to produce it for years to come.

Occasionally, even the best winemakers produce a poor wine. After all, wine is a living product, and sometimes its chemistry takes it in the wrong direction through no fault of the winemaker. Wineries want to maintain their image and their wallet, so a marketing intervention would be helpful at this juncture. Fortunately, there is a process called distillation. It is not new. The process has been around for centuries.

One year we observed that older vintages of red wines Leon Millot and Chambourcin had declining sales, and the wines were not aging gracefully. So, here we go again, Belted Bartletts #3. We disgorged the remaining pallets of these rogue wines. We contracted their distillation with a nearby distillery, placed the distilled wine into small new white oak barrels, and waited two years (a legal condition for it to be called brandy). We were rewarded for our patience with delicious brandy, which we sold for $34 a bottle.

TWENTY-SIX

Please Buy My Ida Reds

*The importance of growing the right
farm commodity cannot be overemphasized.*

FARMING CAN BE A VERY SPIRITUAL OCCUPATION. THE PUBlisher of this book asked me to expand upon the previous sentence, so I engaged with the internet to see what I could find out about the relationship between farming and agricultural spirituality. I did not realize I had touched upon a subject that has been analyzed for centuries. I quickly concluded that I did not feel qualified to delve into this subject matter. However, when I googled "farming and spirituality," I did find this: *By viewing agriculture through a spiritual lens, we begin to see the act of planting, growing, and harvesting as a form of communion with the divine. It teaches us patience, stewardship, and gratitude, reminding us of our role not as conquerors of the earth but as its caretakers.* ("Embracing the Spiritual Harvest: How Faith and Farming Can Coexist for a Sustainable Future." The Schoolhouse Life, 22 Feb 2024, www.theschoolhouselife.com/blog/faith-farming-sustainable-future)

And now, moving on to what I was going to say: to me, planting seeds or trees or fostering a day-old calf through its life is highly rewarding. I don't need cocaine to feel high. My brain fills with serotonin on a regular basis, just watching a corn seed poke through the soil or a peach bud morph into its pink blossom. I know this sounds corny to the casual reader, but it is true. Everyone should have the experience of planting a tree and watching it grow.

Selecting the right agricultural commodity is one of the most important decisions a farmer will make. A farmer may have a certain affinity to plant a particular tree variety, but their yield must have a buyer. A farmer can no longer decide to plant an acre of Red Delicious just because he likes its color and taste. This would likely be a bad decision. The Red Delicious variety is losing in the competition for customer preference and will be a tough sell five years from now.

In my opinion, a farmer looking to enter the dairy business will likely not do well. The Federal Government sets the minimum price that a farmer can receive for his or her milk. This is called the Federal Market Milk Order, FMMO. As I see it, this minimum price becomes *the* price. If a farmer experiences higher input costs for replacement dairy cows, equipment, labor, or feed, he or she cannot simply raise their milk price because the Milk Order is in effect.

I believe another factor that could disrupt the milk market is plant-based milk, which is slowly replacing the white fatty liquid squeezed from a cow's udder. You will not find any mammal's milk in our refrigerator as it has been replaced with milk from oats, soy, coconut, or almonds. I will, however, occasionally enjoy an ice cream cone. For these reasons alone, a farmer could make a large investment in money and time only to find low demand and poor prices.

In the tree fruit business, I had to constantly evaluate what strains of fruit were in vogue. Consumer preferences are in a constant state of flux. A farmer must put in time researching which fruit strains will likely be popular ten years from now. Not an easy task.

Let me try to drive my point home. I decided to begin planting tree fruit and wine grapes in 1983. I wanted to make an informed decision, so I met with our county extension agent. The outcome of our session pointed me to bosc pears, plums, peaches, apples, and wine grapes. Some of you reading this may be a famous movie star or an NFL football hero, and as such, most likely have an agent. Farmers also have agents at their disposal who assist them with agricultural issues, business planning, and education. Most states provide this service to farmers, and it is funded by taxpayers like you. Thank you!

The plan to be successful with the tree selection is compounded by the fact it can take five to ten years for the trees to be productive. The consumer demand for any one variety can weaken over that span of time. Studies have noted that it takes eleven years for apple trees on M111 rootstock to be profitable. M111 is one of many size-controlling roots available onto which apple trees are grafted. The 111 version yields a mature tree that is eighty-five percent of a full-size tree. An apple's popularity can and does change over time. When you consider that there are 7,500 different apple varieties grown in the world, the selection process becomes a little scary. What will the next sensation be—Ruby Frost, Pink Lady, or Evercrisp? And will the demand for these apples still be strong when my trees kick into high production?

So, let's go back to my selection in 1983. We went heavy into peaches. Peach variety selection is not too critical as it pertains to flavor; people savor all peaches. We, as farmers, simply need to extend the harvest season for as long as possible to satisfy all of our peach lovers. Careful planning and selection of peach strains enabled us to harvest peaches from late June into early October.

We also planted a lot of Bosc pears. The pear market was strong for the first fifteen years, as we would get $20 a box. In 2019, we received $18, so seventeen years later, they were worth less than when we started! The market for New York State-grown pears faded away, a trend I could not have predicted back in 1983. The decision to remove pear trees was not too difficult.

Our decision to plant plums and our selection of their varieties started off strong. We made an informed decision and planted three Japanese strains, including Shiro, Ozark Premier, and Methley. Other area farms were experiencing success with these strains. Once the trees reached maturity, at about five years, the trees began to crop robustly. At about year eight, the Shiro crop was so large that we couldn't sell them all. However, two things changed around year ten. An insect called San Jose Scale got a foothold in the trees' bark, which proved impossible to eradicate, causing the trees' health to decline. The second issue had to do with the fruit set. As the years progressed, we were unable to get the trees to reliably produce a crop, resulting in an erratic revenue stream. It may have had to do with cold winter temperatures or poor pollination conditions. It made sense to remove them and find a more reliable crop.

As I mentioned earlier, wine grapes were part of our initial foray into fruit and away from livestock. We began with the French hybrid Seyval Blanc—those vines now forty years old—followed by many other hybrids. We continuously planted wine grapes to replace any fruit trees being retired as demand for grapes kept rising. It was a no-brainer.

I initiated my apple plan slowly. I did a test planting that included seven rows on M111 rootstock, which produces a large tree. I planted thirteen trees per row on 16' by 22' spacing. My varieties were Ida Red, Jonagold, Lady, Red Delicious, Empire, and Jonamac. Only Lady apples remain from this first planting. Jonamac was the first to go, as these apples tended to be small. Jonagold was next, as the sport I had picked lacked the consumer-desired red color. People tend to buy fruit with their eyes and not their tongue. (Biologically, a sport is a spontaneous mutation that produces offspring with abnormal variation from its parents.) This decision didn't go over too well at home as Jonagold was MaryEllen's favorite apple for pies and applesauce. Red Delicious went next. It was the hot apple for many years, and then it wasn't. Yes, it is very red, but it tastes like cardboard, especially those from Washington state. Empire was eliminated simply because better varieties became available; storability was never its strong suit. That left Ida Red. I grafted half of its row to Northern Spy—another questionable decision as it's a bi-annual cropper. That left me with just six Ida Red trees. It got to the point where I could only sell six bushels a year. Clearly, this apple variety was on its way out. Each weekly sales call ended with, "Would you like to add a bushel of Ida Reds to your order?"

Needless to say, these were also removed and replaced as well as the grafted Northern Spy. I put in a row of Rhode Island Greening, which I could sell because I had found a robust market for green apples! Thoughtful planning and thorough research can minimize investment losses and maximize potential success.

THIRTY-SEVEN

Steer Into the Skid

Driving vehicles on slippery surfaces can be highly stressful events and have unpredictable outcomes. Some situations I have encountered are both humorous and educational.

Farming on the side of a mountain can produce some challenging navigation experiences. Except for our "farmyard," there were no flat areas on our farm, and as such, when there was a need to move from any point on the farm to another, you were either heading up or down to get there. Nearly all of the time, movement about the farm was a non-event. Most tasks involving equipment were done at a speed of two to three mph. Tractor travel on our crude farm roads never exceeded five mph. If we stayed on the farm roads, we experienced a normal heart rhythm, but leaving the roads could, and has, led to some scary events, and I am still here to write about them.

Loss of control is usual when using two-wheel drive tractors. Four-wheel drive tractors have twice the traction of a two-wheel drive and, therefore, are considered safer. All agricultural tractors are assumed to be two-wheel drive machines. In the case of a two-wheel drive tractor, only one rear wheel drives; the other simply rotates on its axle. If a tractor featured a four-wheel drive transmission, it would have a shift lever used to engage gears in the front axle, which adds a drive wheel in the front axle, and as in the rear axle, the other front wheel just rotates on its axle. The bottom line is that the term "four-wheel" drive is deceptive, as only two wheels are propelling the machine. If all four wheels were driving, the machine could not be turned.

A couple of sliding events come to mind. These have to do with loss of traction, usually on wet earth or grass. Sliding around in the snow or on ice is even more unpredictable. If you live in northern climates and drive, you know what I mean. So, what do I mean by saying, "Steer into the skid"?

For example, let's say you have completed a tractor safety course and have moved about on some farm roads on a John Deere 2150 (make and model not important, just want to make it real) and are now in a field heading down a hill. The hill slopes down due east. You would like to head southeast, so you turn the wheels to head in that direction, but the tractor loses traction and starts sliding sideways to the east. If you took no action, you and the tractor would tip over, tumbling eastward. But if you turned the front wheels back to the east (in the direction of the slide or skid), the tractor would respond and then travel down the hill in an easterly direction. I will admit this entire event would have occurred over the course of about three seconds, so a rapid assessment and response is imperative. Failure to do so will likely lead to an overturned tractor, resulting in serious injury to the operator. This is when Roll-Over Protection Structures, or ROPS, are helpful. These are steel-framed structures built into the tractor for the purpose of keeping the machine from rolling should it tip over. The intent is to keep the operator safely strapped in the seat and avoid being crushed by an overturned tractor. It does, however, require that the operator have the seat belt secured. I suspect that in most accident situations, the ROPS doesn't work because the operator did not use the seat belt.

One of my early sliding episodes involved the John Deere 2150; yes, the same 2150 used in my educational paragraph above. As we planted out the farm after I was laid off from IBM, the perfect sites were used up first. Then, we started squeezing in plantings in less-than-ideal spots. The center portion of our original farm was not suitable for planting as it was too steep; however, the base of one area in the center portion had enough space to plant five rows of Cayuga White wine grapes. The space to its west went immediately uphill. The uphill side had to be mowed twice a year, which I had successfully done with our Ford Orchard 4000 tractor many times. It had a very low center of gravity and, thus, a low probability of tipping over. On this day, for no logical reason that I can recall, I decided to mow with the Deere. Picture the rows of grapes planted at the bottom of the hill perpendicular to the hill slope. On one of the downhill passes, the Deere lost traction and began sliding, heading directly for the grapes. In this case, I would have preferred to steer the tractor left or right, thereby avoiding the grapes; however, if I had chosen that action, the tractor would have surely flipped over, and it would have meant "Goodbye, Dougie," since I wasn't wearing the seatbelt. So, heart in throat, I stayed the course and steered into the skid, taking out a portion of grapes, wire, posts, and pride in the process, but I lived to tell this story.

Recently, I set myself up for another slide. This time, I was mowing a steep section just above the Vidal Blanc grapes. We had gotten abundant rain, and the ground was saturated. And as I write these words, I see the word "saturated" should have been a signal of what not to do. I had the brush hog on the back of the Deere 5083, ready to tame the grassy slope. This tractor had bias ply tires on the rear. I make this note because if you were to analyze the actual tire-to-soil contact area, it would be less than twelve square inches. Essentially, it is the same footprint as two of my size thirteen work boots. Also, remember, a two-wheel drive tractor only has traction to one wheel at any one moment. The entire 3.6 tons of tractor mass was being held to the side of this hill with two of my shoe prints.

Normally, I would mow this area while heading uphill; I can't explain this; it just feels safer. But on this day, again for no logical reason that I recall, I tossed all my wisdom aside and proceeded downhill. I quickly went into a slide. Don't be alarmed; the outcome was okay. I summoned my "how to slide down the hill" knowledge and steered into the skid. I was headed directly into the vineyard, which was, as before, perpendicular to my trajectory. Keep in mind that the slide would consume about four seconds before impact. I encouraged my brain to do something heroic. The hill flattened just a little just before the first row of grapes. My brain sent a message to my hand to raise the brush hog off the ground, thereby placing the half-ton of its weight onto the rear tires. It worked, and the traction returned; I was able to stop before destroying the vineyard, and I was permitted to live another day.

Not all my noteworthy slides occurred on the farm. I remember the details of another event, except this time, I was driving our 1980 Chevy Malibu. This slide had to do with snowy town road conditions. I have an abnormal amount of confidence in my ability to drive in the snow, but I have no confidence whatsoever in those driving near me. I was heading down to the village by way of what is known locally as Manion's Hill. There was a little snow on the road surface, and I had navigated to this point with no issues. The road has a couple of turns, but none are considered remarkable. The last road turn has a forty-five-degree bend to the left. There is a red house at the bottom of the hill, directly in line with the road at the start of the left turn. The house had to have been constructed before building codes, as it is set back only ten feet from the road edge. I had driven by this house hundreds of times and eventually took notice of its design. Directly attached to the corner of the house is a large concrete buttress, which I had concluded was put there to protect the house. It must have taken ten yards of material to fill the forms. The barrier is directly in line with the road just before it turns left. I could only deduce that the house must have suffered some hits from rogue vehicles during its lifetime.

On this particular day, I found myself driving one of those rogue cars I just mentioned. I was at the top of the hill with the red house in my sight. For reasons which I cannot explain—perhaps a section of black ice—the Malibu began to slide, and then the slide morphed into a slow clockwise spin. Without thinking, my hands tried to turn the wheels in the direction of motion. The only problem was that the direction of motion was continuously changing. I WAS SPINNING and, at one point, was headed directly for the house, going backward! In those brief seconds, I thought there was no way I was getting out of this situation gracefully. There was not much I could do except ride it out. I am not a particularly religious man, but some force greater than me must have stepped in. At the base of the hill, precisely at the beginning of the forty-five-degree turn and immediately following the completion of one full, 360-degree revolution, the car resumed normal road control, and I continued my trip to the village as if the whole spin routine had never happened. My "steer into the skid' advice saved me from injury and embarrassment.

TWENTY-EIGHT

Day Trading

There may be other ways of making some money while farming; day trading in the stock market is not likely one of them.

DAY TRADING IS A FINANCIAL TERM THAT INVOLVES BUYING and selling stocks over short periods of time, specifically within one day. My definition is a little looser as I would hold stocks for one day but more often for months. I bring this concept to light because some of my farmer friends are engaged in day trading. To be fair, most of them buy and hold stocks, which is the method proven to have the most successful results. Some may view day trading as gambling.

Farming is not a whole lot different than gambling. It really doesn't matter what kind of agriculture a farmer chooses. When you think about it, farmers are professional gamblers. Farmers know that during any one year, a weather event can occur, resulting in little profit and, more likely, a loss. Most of our losses were associated with cold temperatures or hail. Other areas of the county will suffer losses due to drought, floods, wildfires, and hurricanes. Insects and diseases also do their part each year to challenge a successful harvest. Even after harvest, agricultural commodity prices can experience wide fluctuations.

In reality, it is not a huge leap from farmer to day trader. The 1990s was the dot-com era, during which there was a consistently large volume of day trading. A wave of companies were "going public" to be listed on a Stock Exchange through an official procedure called an Initial Public Offering or IPO, and their stock prices would experience wild swings. These young companies had high expectations, no proven record, and were nearly always losing money. In any one trading week, a company's stock price could double or be sliced in half. Everyone was trying to buy low and sell high. People in the financial world will tell you that one cannot reliably make a profit day trading, but that didn't dissuade me. My farmer friends and I would share stock picks and tips. It was exciting to try to pick the next IBM, Microsoft, or Nvidia. My knowledge about the world of stock trading did expand during this period. I learned about "puts" and "calls," EBITDA (Earnings Before Interest Tax Depreciation and Amortization), inverted yield curve, price-to-book ratio, and ETFs (Electronically Traded Funds). To be honest, even though I had a broader understanding of the stock market, I don't believe any of this made a difference. When I look back at this period, I am pretty sure I made no profit. This is not to say that people don't make money via day trading, but for the average person, profit via day trading is an elusive quest.

Stock market "investing" is a different story. All one really has to do is select a few solid, low-expense ratio index funds. Add some dollars to them over time on a regular basis, don't panic in a stock market dip, never sell them, and wait thirty years. This would be termed "investing," and I know for a fact that this strategy works.

Now that I am in retirement mode (and you're not going to believe this), I am day trading! When Covid-19 struck in March of 2020, I couldn't resist the market dip; maybe a buying opportunity?

I moved a small amount of money to an online trading account and have been trading ever since. I will admit that my goals are different than they were in the 90s. Of course, I am still seeking profit, but this time around, the quest includes knowledge, and unlike when I was farming 24/7, I have the luxury of time to spend at the computer. It is stimulating to research the companies I pick, especially those considered tech. I now have a better understanding of MRNA, solid-state batteries, and farming under glass. I should mention here that my trading account does not represent a meaningful portion of our overall net worth, and if I perform poorly, we could still take a nice vacation. And, oh yes, I have been told by MaryEllen that I cannot add to it. Only time will tell if my trading ends with success, but at least the journey is satisfying.

TWENTY-NINE

Negotiation

The process of negotiation is often employed during a farm career. Some situations are highlighted here to make the point.

THE ART OF NEGOTIATION HAS BEEN AROUND FOR THOUSANDS of years. It is clearly not a new concept. I am talking about how one decides what something is worth. Suppose Fred Flintstone needed a new stone tire for his cavemobile. How was it decided what it should cost? Was the prehistoric currency some quantity of reptile teeth, or could Fred perhaps negotiate a trade of ten dozen dinosaur eggs for the tire?

Farmers are involved with hundreds of purchases and sales in any one year. Some things are simply not negotable. When you are at the gasoline pump, and it says $3.29 per gallon, you are not likely to stroll into the attendant's office and say, "Will you take three bucks?"

However, in the case of farming, it seems as though every third transaction is a negotiation. Try going to your auto parts store; you bring a part for your snowplow to the register and ask, "How much is this skid disk?" The agent says, "It will be $33.95." And I say, "But I have an account here." His response is, "Oh, in that case, it will be $27.95." The new agent did not recognize me sporting my new white beard, so I had to speak up. A small negotiation.

The Farm Bureau magazine *Grassroots* arrives in the mail. You read through the headlines and bitch to your wife about new regulations and taxes being proposed by state bureaucrats. A few more pages are turned, and you calm down. You soon get to the ad section and casually read through them, and you see that John Deere 14T baler you would like to have. You have had yours for thirty years, and just this past summer, you paid for three service calls to keep it baling. The advertised baler is located at a farm about an hour away. You inspect your truck hitch, verify the checkbook balance with the farm accounting department—your wife—in case you should consummate the deal, and off you go. You drive over to the farm, do your inspection, and decide the purchase will solve your dilemma. Both of you know the baler's approximate value, so you dicker back and forth and make a deal. Another negotiation. It happens every day in farming.

Most farms that grow apples sell much of their fruit through a broker. Large farms may produce 500,000 bushels in any one year. It would be super challenging to move that much fruit through their road stand. Our farm was considered small, and we were able to market most fruit via direct sales, so I was able to avoid a broker situation in most years. I had spent considerable time seeking out and developing prospective markets, which included small stores, roadside stands, Community Supported Agriculture (CSA) programs, other farms, and schools. My products were of high quality, and I provided great service. No customer was too small; I would take orders for two boxes or fifty. I did not ask the buyer what he or she would give me per unit; I would tell them the price I needed. This allowed me to be a "price giver." I had a good idea about what my product was worth in my market and mostly got what I wanted. This is not the case in the broker model. I found that when dealing with a fruit broker, you are stuck being a "price taker." You found out how much you would receive when the broker's check arrived, which was often three months after the fruit's delivery. Most often, the price received was underwhelming. On occasion, the farmer may benefit by pushing back with a broker. For example, you know what it costs to produce that bushel of apples, and you need more per unit to be successful. You call your broker up and say, "Sam, I really need $1.50 more per bushel." The usual response from Sam is, "Well, the national crop was very large this year, and we are competing with Washington and Michigan, but I'll see what I can do." A week later, Sam calls back to tell the farmer that his next delivery will be $0.75 per bushel higher. Only through negotiation does the farmer get a better price.

Since selling our fruit farm, I have been trying to be helpful to the new owners. They recognized that I may be of some use in the capacity of a consultant. There are numerous aspects to owning a farm that are not readily understood. The new owner might ask, "Why did you decide to plant the Cabernet Franc vines on riparia rootstock?" or "Where does the main trunk irrigation line travel across the farm?" Or maybe, "What price should I be charging for Granny Smith apples?" Answers to these questions can enhance knowledge, avert mishaps, or improve profits. The role of consultant has value. I ended up trading answers to these kinds of questions for one year's worth of fuel for our new farm. The agreement was reached by negotiation.

Is it possible to conduct a barter deal—a negotiation—without a written contract and without a spoken word? During the calendar year 2022, I renovated a 960-square-foot building that had been previously used as a migrant labor camp on our retirement farm. It had been vacant for four years, and my initial assessment revealed the need for a few minor upgrades. The town code enforcement officer was consulted, and he concluded that the building could be reactivated as farm labor housing so long as I brought it up to the electric code and consulted the county board of health. An electrician was hired, and the first order of business was to install a new electric service entrance. They had not been on the job for more than an hour when my cell phone buzzed—my hearing is awful, and the vibration feature helps to notify me about incoming calls. The electrician calmly said to me, "I think you may have a termite problem; my drill bit passed through the six-inch sill plate in three seconds." I arrived at the site, did a little poking around, and he was right; the sill core was just cellulose dust. Upon further inspection, I concluded that most of the sills, floor joist ends, and half of the wall studs had to be replaced or repaired. Within a couple of days, I initiated the repair process.

The termite issue was the tip of the iceberg; other building deficiencies soon surfaced. Along the way, I also had to dust off some of my dormant tradesman skill set, which included plumber, mason, excavator operator, electrician, and, of course, carpenter. Up to this point, I employed no additional help other than the electrician, as I was attempting to keep the project cost below $15,000. However, I arrived at a point where the termite repair effort was going to be more than my seventy-four-year-old body was willing to take on. The west end of the camp was going to require that all the floor joists be replaced. I contacted my builder friend, Andy, and he gave me a price of $2,500 to make the repairs. He arrived one hot August day with his crew and made the building whole again. Months passed, and I never received a bill. As I write this, it is now March, seven months after the completed work. I am an honest person and always pay my bills, but I didn't have one to pay; one was never sent. What should I do? I pondered my situation a little longer and came to the following conclusion. A year earlier, after clearing our farm of apple trees, I had accumulated ten cords of firewood. I gave all of it to Andy with no expected reciprocation. Months later, a business acquaintance of mine was planning to build a new home. I suggested that he contact Andy to handle the coordination of the construction effort, and Andy got the contract. I concluded that Andy was trading his one day of camp repair work for firewood and maybe the contract lead. This negotiation took place without one word spoken, no words placed on paper, and no emails or texts exchanged. Neither of us has brought up the subject since.

There is a phrase I learned from my farmer friend Frank when I was fourteen. He said, "The person who speaks of money first is the loser." I have carried this thought with me throughout my life. Whenever Frank was trying to buy something that was negotiable, he would try to get the other person to say what they wanted for it. So, let's say a neighboring farmer had a finished, corn-fed, black Angus steer for sale. Frank wanted to buy it, and both men knew the approximate weight of the steer. In Frank's mind, he was willing to pay $1.35 per pound, but he was not going to let those words leave his lips. He let the seller speak first, and when he said, "I need $1.00 per pound," Frank said okay. He saved thirty-five cents per pound just by keeping his mouth shut.

You can apply this strategy in many situations. I have found it quite useful in my negotiations.

THIRTY

The List

A list can be helpful in completing daily and seasonal tasks. Achieving daily goals can be inspiring.

Do you make lists? I do and have done so for forty years. I have found that I don't function well without them. For a very brief period, I attempted to do without one and just go with the flow of the day. A week passed, and I found that tasks were not getting done, and I felt a bit directionless. The list soon returned, and all was well with the world.

I have two versions of the lists. One is created daily, seven days a week, at breakfast. It is done on a scrap of paper about 3x5 inches. This list defines what needs to be done during that day. The number of entries will vary, usually from three to fifteen items. When I was farming full-time, the tasks might have included: call Jake, deliver school apples, rack white wine, bottle Seyval, order irrigation supplies, or change Ford tractor oil. Occasionally, a rogue entry would appear. MaryEllen would add an item when I stepped away from the table. It would be something like: water the flowers, kiss your wife, or pet the puppy dog before you leave for the day. I always made sure to complete those items. These days my daily list items might be: mow the lawn, weed the garden, sucker the grapes, and pull and rack the garlic. I revisit the daily list from time to time during the day to monitor my progress. Entries get crossed out as they are executed, and new items can get added as the day moves along.

I keep the daily list in my top left pocket. I have always worn shirts with a pocket. If there was no pocket, there would be nowhere to put the list. Hot summer days are a problem as I will perspire, causing the gel pen ink to smudge and render the entries mostly illegible.

Toward the end of the day, I will review the list to determine if everything got accomplished. I have, at times, done something during a day that was not on the list. If the task had some significance, I would add it to the list and then immediately cross it out. Am I insane? Not really. As I have alluded to in this book, farming offers a lot of visual feedback. Basking in momentary daily successes is stimulating and satisfying. It was easy to feel good about the hundred baskets of peaches you had just brought in from the orchard or finishing trimming a 330-foot-long row of grapes. Completing the list is no different. It's like achieving many mini-successes all day long.

The second version of my list, the "master list," is longer, the entries consume more time to achieve, and they don't get done today. The items on this list may get done this week or this year. Some don't get done at all. The paper it's written on is larger as well, usually 5x8 inches, and it won't fit in my pocket without three folds, but that doesn't matter because this list generally stays next to my place at the kitchen table. Before retirement, items on this list might have included: install grape posts, erect new deer fence, plan new peach orchard, or research growing mushrooms. I also employ a priority or urgency scale. It is a one-, two- and three-star notation system. The most urgent tasks can get three

In These Veins

DEMPSEY STEEL PIPE CO.

511 RT. 17K (COLDENHAM) – WALDEN, NY 12586
(845) 564-1230   FAX: (845) 564-1232
www.dempseysteelpipe.com

```
change 2150 oil                    get quote - crush pad
** get deer fence quote            *** bottle Sauvual
assess fertilyzer needs            taste through red wines
pound grape post                   review marketing plan
chop brush                         *** find more farm help
* replace dead vines               review wine pricing
trim apple                         research CF clones
fix barn roof leak                 get nuisance permit
* order irrigation supplies        *** file business taxes
new tires for Sierra               ** repair TN hydraulic hose
get flatbed inspection             ** repair 4430 AC
order bamboo stakes                sharpen 80" mower
** burn brush piles                weld brush hog deck
tension grape wires                *** clean crush pad sump
remove 1 row Ida Red               research pressure washer
conduct apple trim demo.           regrade farm road
*** rake grape brush               assess weed control
support new apple trees            * assess apple thin strategy
repair 5083 tach                   paint farm bathroom
```

STEEL PIPE – NEW & USED   **WELD FITTINGS & FLANGES**
STEEL CULVERT & PLASTIC CULVERT **DRESSER COUPLINGS**

The list

stars and never more. Items are added and crossed out just like on the daily list. The list gets rebooted when the paper is filled.

I still use lists in my retirement. The master list is still just as long, though its content is a little different. It might include things like: plan corvette trip, decide next vacation, or order spring seeds. The daily list has been shorter, but the satisfaction of accomplishment hasn't changed. If you've never used lists before, I encourage you to try them. It feels good!

THIRTY-ONE

The Farm Wife

*Reflections on the role of a farm wife,
how to find and keep one.*

DO YOU THINK A FARMER CAN BE SUCCESSFUL WITHOUT A wife? I believe most farmers would answer no. In addition to the activities already mentioned, a wife fills many roles on the family farm. Of course, there are the usual weekly tasks like food shopping, cooking, cleaning, and laundry, but classically, a farmer's wife takes on much more. The wife often handles the mail, manages banking, and does the "books." She will also go get the fuel filter for the John Deere, receive fruit orders, and call your brother back. She will pack fruit with you late into the night to satisfy an urgent order long after the help has gone for the day and then pilot the standard transmission truck to eight stops spanning three counties. Need a birthday card for Mother? Just ask, and she will scour the rack for the perfect wording.

Of course, all of us like to "get lucky" from time to time, often when we are younger and less likely when we are older. Invariably, planning either will or doesn't work, and babies are born. What's a farm without children? Raising a young family is a full-time job. The wife will often do more than her fair share of child-rearing.

A farm wife is also a business partner. MaryEllen and I have had countless conversations and analysis sessions about what to grow, where to market our fruit, and what a good capital investment is. We've also had many conversations about how best to move forward when a project doesn't go as planned. We've brainstormed our way into and out of many life adventures. We haven't always agreed, and we've become very good at debating and embracing the art of compromise. Each of us has learned what's important to the other, when we should push hard to get our way, and when we should give in.

A little side story here. Back in the early days, after MaryEllen pointed out that she helped take care of my Labrador Retriever, Tamara, the pigs, the cows, and the barn cats but didn't have a pet of her own, I brought home a chocolate Labrador Retriever puppy for her which she named Kyla. This cute pup worked hard to keep up with Tamara and learn the ways of farm life, but we learned when she was quite young that she had severe hip dysplasia. It limited her endurance somewhat for active farm life, but she was game for anything, and she took breaks as needed. She was very much attached to MaryEllen. One morning out at the barn, as the dogs waited with me while I gave the farm crew instructions, Kyla saw MaryEllen come out the front door of the house as she was leaving for work. Kyla raced toward MaryEllen, and as she headed up the incline on the front lawn, she caught one of her back feet on the ground. She cried out in pain and fell in a lump. Long story short, Kyla had torn her ACL. Surgery to repair it was priced at $1500. Our checking and savings accounts weren't too robust back then. When I heard the cost, I said, "I wonder what the number is where you say that's too much, and you put the dog down." MaryEllen put a flattened hand up in front of her as if to push me back, looked me straight in the eye, and calmly said, "You know, in marriage, you have to pick the fights you want to win. You shouldn't pick this one because you'll lose." I decided that MaryEllen would have the final say in making decisions about our dogs. I would push hard on other things.

Not all women are cut out to be farm wives. When you consider that only two percent of the U.S. population is currently associated with agriculture, how is a woman going to know what to expect in a farm marriage? Seeking out a farmer's daughter might be a good strategy.

But let's say the farmer's daughter route is not in the cards. How do you paint a picture of farm life to a potential wife? Farming is not like most occupations because the business of agriculture is a lifestyle. Do you try to explain to the maybe bride-to-be that there is no weekly paycheck? Most small fruit and vegetable farmers get paid after the harvest, after all the invoice checks come in, and after all the accounts payable are satisfied. They simply take in what's left over, leaving some years better than others. Do you even attempt to broach the possibility of a weather event that leaves the farm without a profit?

How do you dance around the concept of vacation? One- or two-day getaways might be arranged. But a week away during the growing or harvest season is not likely to happen. Case in point, MaryEllen and I had to wait until November 7 to get married—after all the fruit was harvested and the pigs went to market.

On a more positive note, when you consider U.S. statistics, the divorce rate for farm marriages is forty percent less than the national average. There must be something good about life on the farm. Farmers and their wives are partners 24/7 in life and in business. If you can get by these conversations and the girl says okay, you may have a winner.

MaryEllen and I have been happily married for thirty years. I think we are going to make it!

MaryEllen

THIRTY-TWO

Who Shot the Deer?

An unusual winter day event in the orchard.

WHITE-TAILED DEER ARE VERY ABUNDANT IN OUR AREA. The average person—like my wife—may enjoy watching the deer, but to farmers like myself, they are nothing more than rodents. The arrival of winter signals the end of the previous three seasons of deer grazing on grasses. Snow classically arrives in mid-December and can, in some winters, cover the orchard floors until late March. Once the snow arrives, the deer diet switches to bud browsing, and their favorite is apples. Each bud on a tree will produce an apple. Every bite by the deer reduces the fall harvest potential. Winter is three months in duration like all the other seasons, but it seems longer, and during this time, deer can eliminate half of the anticipated new crop. When this happens, it moves the farm's balance sheet from profit to loss. This paragraph is written in the present tense because all of it is true today.

During the other three seasons, we would see deer one to three at a time, but during the winter months, they tended to pack up. Most of the orchards on our farm were not visible from the house, so they were able to browse to their hearts' content, and I would never see them. The barn lot orchard to the south of the house, however, was in plain sight from my kitchen chair. I would tolerate the browsing for a while, but eventually, I had to intervene. I tried all the usual deterrent tactics, like hanging soap bars or a bag of mothballs on tree branches, which classically do not work.

I applied for a nuisance permit each year which allowed me to shoot the offending deer. The New York State Department of Environmental Conservation will allow farmers to remove deer out of season once they have proven that they are experiencing economic hardship. To do that, a DEC officer would visit the farm and do a visual inspection of the trees.

In one particular year, we had accumulated a foot and a half of snow. This always ratchets up the tree bud browsing pressure. It was just shy of noon one day, and there were several deer in the barn lot orchard. I fetched my Winchester 270 rifle, fitted with a Simmons variable power scope. I snuck quietly down to the north edge of the orchard, took aim, and dropped one. It fell in place, so I knew it was a solid shot. I decided to let it lay and head inside for lunch. Less than an hour later, I went out to finish my business with the deer. I found the deer, but a short distance away, there was another blood trail. The first thing that entered my mind was, *Who was hunting here while I was gone?* I followed the trail and found dead deer number two. It took a few moments, but I put the puzzle together and realized no one was there in my absence. I had shot both deer with one shot; I just hadn't seen the second deer. They simply happened to line up one directly behind the other so that the single bullet passed through deer number one and into deer number two. I would consider this to be very efficient hunting.

We tolerated the browsing deer for thirty years, but the damage became too challenging. Each year, I lamented the loss of crop potential and its income had the deer not consumed it. We later installed the ultimate solution, an eight-foot-high steel fence, around forty acres of orchard at a cost of $35,000. The browsing ceased, and profits normalized. The excluded deer were now free to bother some other farmer.

THIRTY-THREE

A New Apple

This chapter talks about a farmer's decision process in bringing a new apple variety to the farm.

LET'S SAY YOU HAVE JUST VISITED YOUR FAVORITE ROADSIDE farm stand or perhaps the local farmer's market. Many Americans make a weekly trip to these venues, seeking out the current harvest of fruits and vegetables. They feel good about knowing where their food comes from and how the food is produced, and can often talk to the grower; this interaction puts a face behind the bunch of beets you're going to take home with you. During your visit, perhaps the owner or attendant convinces you to taste a new apple variety. You take home this new-to-you apple, try it that evening in your salad, and you love it! Have you ever thought about what it took to get this new fruit to the market shelf?

Just the process of releasing a new apple variety, also known as a cultivar, can take ten to twenty years. This is often the job of a land grant college and is orchestrated by a plant breeder. Every state has a land grant institution; for New York, it is Cornell University in Ithaca. The breeder is asked to find something better or different than the other 7,000 varieties that are grown around the globe, a very challenging charge. He or she must consider a multitude of factors, including disease resistance, cold hardiness, when it ripens, ease of growing, and most importantly, will the customer love it? There have been some blockbuster releases in the last sixty years. A great example is the sweet, juicy Honeycrisp variety, which is the result of a cross between Macoun and Honeygold. It was released by the University of Minnesota in 1974. It took some time to gain traction but is now heading to be the most popular apple in the country. The Fuji apple, a cross between Red Delicious and Rawls Jennet, was released a little earlier in 1962 from Japan and has gained considerable popularity as well. Cornell University in Geneva, NY, released two promising varieties in 2013: SnapDragon and Ruby Frost. Only time will tell just how popular these newbies will become.

 I have planted some of these new releases as well as varieties simply new to our farm. Regardless of whether the apple is new on the scene or antique, the planning process is the same. The first action is to place a tree order. Let's say I decide to plant the new variety Evercrisp. It is, in fact, my personal favorite at the moment. In the quiet winter months, I make my inquiries with tree nurseries. I place my order, but I am told delivery will be in two years. The days of finding immediate inventory are gone. The nursery will custom bud graft the trees to order, and the process simply takes two years.

 In the meantime, I review our farm layout to determine where the trees can be planted. In the year before the trees arrive, I'll perform soil tests to verify nutrient levels and pH. Wet areas will be tiled to remove excess water. Underground irrigation infrastructure is verified or added. I verify that I have enough money for this venture, as the cost of a new orchard is about $20,000 per acre. During summer and fall, based on the results of the soil tests, I will add any deficient nutrients and lime. The ground will be disked multiple times to break down the sod, then spring toothed smooth.

In the spring of the trees' arrival, I establish my planting matrix, first on paper and then in the field. When the soil is ready, the holes are augured, and trees are planted. Soon after, a metal pole is added for each tree, and a wire trellis system is added to each row to stabilize the trees. After this point, most of the farmer's effort in this first year of the tree's life is spent watching the trees grow. When the tree arrives from the nursery, it's four feet tall. It will grow two to four feet in its first year while the roots below the soil surface get acclimated to their new growing medium. I will mow the orchard middles and try to keep the tree rows weed-free. Fall arrives, then winter, which allows the trees to sleep. An apple tree must experience 500 to 1,000 hours below forty-five degrees Fahrenheit to successfully flourish in a particular climate. This is called chill hours and can vary greatly among varieties.

Spring arrives, and another cycle begins. This is the second year of the young trees' life on our farm, but we are four years into the planning cycle, and not one dollar has come in. All blossoms are plucked off the tree as we want all the tree's energy allocated to growing new wood and more roots. A light crop protectant program is implemented to keep diseases like scab and fire blight at bay. Grass and weed management continues. The trees will grow another four feet, and most should reach their target height of twelve feet. At the end of this fourth year of our journey, we have about $25,000 invested in an acre of Evercrisp. I sure hope people will want these apples.

Year five comes around. This is the money year. We hope there will be no winter nights at negative twelve degrees or spring freezes that will take out the precious buds or blossoms. May comes around, ample bees visit the flowers to perform their pollination magic, and we are on our way. We might even have to thin off some fruit to attain the maximum size of individual fruits.

The crop protectant program will need tweaking as now insects will want to sample the fruit.

The prize is within our sight. If luck is on our side this year, it won't hail, and when the healthy crop is ready to be harvested, we'll be fortunate to find enough pickers. There are no robots available for the picking job, although the technology is in the wings. Every single apple is picked one at a time by a human hand. The crop is successfully harvested, sorted, packaged, and shipped to Whole Foods, Hannaford, and Price Chopper.

Five years have passed since we made our decision to plant a new apple, and now judgment day is here. Is my favorite apple, Evercrisp, still popular, or did another consumer whim sneak in during the wait? Did we make the right decision, and will you love my new apple as much as I do?

THIRTY-FOUR

Iowa Chief

There is a certain segment of our society that can't wait for the new seed catalogs to arrive each year. I talk about why and how their arrival sparks excitement and potential for the new year.

SEED CATALOGS HAVE BEEN AROUND FOR OVER A HUNDRED years. Catalog names like Burpee, Gurney, Harris, and Johnny's come to mind. They arrive in the mail starting in mid-December and flow into early January, just as we are about to enter the heart of winter. Some catalogs will carry lifelike photos of the mature plant and their bounty. There is a temptation to order a little of everything your eye passes over. It is as if spring is just around the corner, and the potential of a new year is near.

Seed varieties do disappear from catalogs from time to time. Just like with apples, some of the older favorites fall out of favor and are replaced by newer versions. New varieties may have sweeter fruit, better flavor, unique color, or ripen early. The retired seed may become an heirloom variety. When I was growing up in the 1960s, Iowa Chief sweet corn was popular. It was a small kernel, large-eared, eighty-six days to harvest, yellow corn with great flavor, so I planted it faithfully for many seasons. Over time, it became difficult to find, and I was forced to find an alternative. I moved to bi-colored ears of white and yellow kernels, which I found to be quite satisfying. Larger catalogs may contain up to twenty varieties of a particular vegetable. The loss of an old favorite is not the end of the world. The bounty of choices, however, can make you a little dizzy when deciding which one to select.

Most of the seeds in these catalogs end up in our American gardens. We tend to order small packets or maybe as much as a pound. Small farms may also use the same catalog but will order a pound of small seed and ten to twenty pounds of larger seed at any one time. I tend to order about 1,000 seeds of small plants like Swiss chard or radishes and a pound of something like bush beans. I stagger multiple plantings of each variety so I can have a continuous harvest throughout the summer. I have had a garden for fifty-four consecutive years. They usually measure 50' by 50'. A lot of food can be grown in that 2,500 square feet. Often, by the third week in July, the daily harvest exceeds our consumption rate, so MaryEllen will process some of the bounty into our freezer, or we will offer the excess to appreciative neighbors who don't have gardens.

The difference between going to a grocery store for vegetables or harvesting them from your garden is freshness. Freshly picked vegetables from the garden simply taste better. Many summer suppers that MaryEllen serves were in the garden two hours prior. In the case of sweet corn, she will get a pot of water boiling as I hurry to the garden to get the corn. It's on our plates ten minutes later.

I have grown nearly every vegetable variety listed in a typical seed catalog. I did say nearly. This spring, I'll be trying kale and hardscape garlic for the first time, and I will be bringing back white and red potatoes, which I haven't grown since the early '70s.

MaryEllen recently purchased an air fryer with which she prepares red-skinned potatoes, among other vegetables. They are to die for!

In a way, perhaps our gardens are micro-farms. Only two percent of Americans are associated with agriculture, but I suspect many of you would like to be a farmer. It really is a good life. We start to dream about having chickens, cows, sheep, and rabbits and perhaps a few acres of grapes, tomatoes, and raspberries or Christmas trees, but once the planning process commences, reality tends to set in. It will take a sizable initial financial investment, and a reliable regular paycheck is not likely to happen. A garden can fulfill some of these farming desires at a much lower risk.

It seems that opportunities for me to plant something keep popping up. There is a plot of land just south of our new house. There had been an orchard there in prior years. The land had been renovated during its previous ownership but not done well. The earth's surface was uneven, rutted, punctuated by numerous rocks, and difficult to maintain. In the spring of 2022, I decided to tame the unruly field. I made an initial pass with my bucket loader to remove the obvious rocks. It was then plowed, followed by numerous passes with a disk and then a harrow, eventually achieving the smooth surface I was looking for. I decided to plant it with orchard grass as it is well suited for New York State growing conditions. It wasn't going to be pastured or cut for hay. As I have spoken of in other chapters, this is a retirement farm, and it does not need to make a profit, so we can make what may turn out to be bad decisions but with no significant monetary consequences. However, there is a benefit, in the eyes of the town assessor, to maintaining a parcel of land as a farm. From a financial perspective, if we can gross $10,000 per year (profit not important), we can keep our land tax farm exemption, so we planted 2,000 wine grapevines to harvest and sell grapes to ultimately achieve that goal. Another benefit could be simply viewing what we grow. So, picking up from a couple sentences ago, we decided to plant the orchard grass for the sole purpose of watching the ripe grass fronds dance to the beat of light winds passing over them. We just wanted to create visual texture in our viewshed. We name all our fields; this one is called Magic Meadow.

Magic Meadow's soil was finally ready for its seeding, but the soil stayed too wet with constant rain showers, and I missed the spring planting window. Spring turned into summer, and then it was too hot and dry for good germination. My next opportunity would be late summer to early fall. I called my farmer friend Frank, and he confirmed my thoughts about timing. The calendar rolled over to late August, and I was ready, but my plans were dashed by an approaching hurricane. It arrived, releasing six inches of rain. Now, the field was too wet again. Ten days passed, and the field was ready once more. But now, another hurricane was approaching, and I had a decision to make. Do I plant before the rain and risk a washout, or wait until after the rain and risk compromised germination conditions? Grass germinates best at seventy degrees Fahrenheit and needs ten to fourteen days to do so. The days were now turning shorter and cooler. This was getting to be stressful, and it felt like I was farming again. I had retired for the sole purpose of shucking responsibility and the associated stress.

I decided to seed before the rains and take my chances with washouts. The second hurricane arrived as expected and dropped five more inches of rain. Now we were back to farming! All the variables of weather were surfacing. Mother Nature was doing her thing; there was a risk of failure, and we may lose all I had invested, just like old times.

I waited for ten days but didn't see the anticipated green hue emanating from the soil. I got nervous and reordered the seed. MaryEllen thought she saw the hue, but I didn't. A couple more days passed, and no hue. Each morning, as MaryEllen and I met at the kitchen sink after breakfast, she asked, "Do you see any green down there?" glancing out at the field. I answered, "No, do you?"

For the first week, she agreed with me. Then, one morning, she responded simply, "Yup, I think so. Can't you see it?" With my ever-hopeful farmer heart, I kept searching for any sign of a green tinge in the barren landscape, but it just wasn't there. It became kind of a daily joke between us. As positive as MaryEllen was that she could see green in the field, I was just as positive that it wasn't there and the effort had been a failure. I may have mentioned before that I do not accept failure without a fight. My analytical brain kicked in, which caused me to research what really goes on in the germination process. Come to find out, the first phase of seed germination is called imbibition. It is the process of taking on moisture. It allows the seed to swell, thereby allowing follow-on processes of the seed's development to occur. We humans are familiar with the term "to imbibe," as in taking on alcohol. The seed is just going to take on a little water, and we'll leave it there.

Armed with this knowledge, I felt renewed hope. We certainly had ample moisture. But my impatience naturally pushed me to take it a little further, and I have done this before. I headed down to the field, got down on my hands and knees, and crawled around a bit, doing some scratching through the crusted, rain-compressed earth with my pocket knife. Keep in mind, these seeds are very small and hard to see—barely an eighth inch long and a fat horsehair wide—I did find some tiny threads of yellow just below the surface. These infant seed sprouts would shortly break the earth's cover and turn green once the sun's light hit them. Success was just around the bend! A few more days passed, and the green hue finally began to appear. My anxiety melted away. A month later, our new field was completely green. By next May, the grass would be three feet tall and gently swaying in the wind.

As I mentioned earlier, I was considering the project a total failure, and I had ordered another bag of orchard grass seed, planning to plant the field again the following spring. As I said, I don't like failure, and my philosophy is I will not be beaten. If the grass wouldn't grow this year, I could make it happen next year. Besides, if Magic Meadow did green up, I could prep another field to sow orchard grass and go through the whole process again. Naturally, I would look forward to it.

I highly recommend you seek out a seed catalog or a few packets of seed. You will be rewarded!

THIRTY-FIVE

Railroad in the Woods

*Tale of the Underground Railroad
and what woods mean to me.*

How do we distinguish between folklore and historical fact? I am sure all towns in our country have at least a handful of tales, folklore, and even legends passed down through the decades. I suppose stories remain tales if their content can't be corroborated.

The westernmost section of our former farm is wooded, populated with mostly black oak and hemlock trees, occupying about ten acres. It sits on one of the highest points in our town at 850' elevation. The view at its east side boasts a panoramic vista twenty miles wide and equally deep, extending over the Hudson River toward the Taconic Mountain range in Dutchess County. The area immediately west of our woods is simply more dense woods, and there is nothing back there. Tracing our ridgeline south will bring you to Newburgh and to the north to Kingston, covering a distance of thirty-five miles. The ridgeline is pierced from time to time by various town or county east-west roads and is generally lightly inhabited. There are no official roads enabling easy north-south travel; however, numerous trails and logging roads can be pieced together to navigate the ridge. Although I have not done it, I can visualize someone making the thirty-five-mile trek, never to be noticed.

Our neighbor Patricia Stewart, a lifelong resident of Marlboro, would fill us in intermittently about local history and folklore. Sometimes, there would be years of gaps in our exchanges. Recalling conversations with her always brings a smile as she would pick up a conversation as if we last spoke just yesterday, not missing a beat. Patricia's family owned an eight-acre wood lot directly north of ours. In one of our discussions, she relayed to me the story of an Underground Railroad station as it related to her woodlot. She was unable to navigate the woods but did give an adequate description of where to look for the station. My curiosity was piqued to flesh out her tale. Obviously, this was not any ordinary station with railroad tracks passing by some sort of physical structure. I hiked up to the spot described, and at first view, there was nothing to see. No casual passerby would stop in awe to view "the station."

I studied the trees and rocks, looking for clues. The site sat adjacent to an old logging road. As I alluded to above, these makeshift roads and paths could easily be patched together to provide a secluded passage under the canopy of the forest's tall oak trees' leaves and branches. Ten feet to the west of the road, I found remains of what could have been a stone foundation. Without too much difficulty, I could piece together the perimeters. There was an opening in the stone, which suggested a doorway. Let's call this "the house" for lack of a better description. Immediately to the north, I located more rock remnants, positioned in straight lines, intersecting others, also forming perimeters of another closed space. The rock arrangement was way too straight to have been put there by the last glacier. Some humans had to have done this. This space was much larger and could have likely been a corral for horses. Immediately to the west of the corral was another deposit of placed rocks, suggesting a second corral.

I sought out other evidence to firm up Patricia's tale but found none. If this was an Underground Railroad station, it would have been in use sometime during the period from 1830 to 1860. Electricity had not arrived yet, so there would be no remnants of copper wire lying about. I could find nothing that would suggest remains of a water well. This does not surprise me as a station such as this would seldom be used, and water could easily be found in ponds and streams along the paths. I hope to get back to the site to do some light archaeology work, perhaps to discover a coin, a piece of pottery, or a door hasp to lend more credibility to the tale. For now, though, we will have to hand down this story as local folklore, waiting to see if more evidence will surface to turn it into history. In the meantime, the tale is alive and well, living in seclusion in the safety and cover of the woods.

Woods not only provide cover for an Underground Railroad but are within themselves an entire ecosystem. The terms "woods" and "forests" are often used interchangeably, but it is quite likely we could agree that forests are larger than woods. Forests cover thirty-one percent of the earth's land area, which provides a habitat for many thousands of species of trees, plants, animals, insects, and fungi. The species take and give within this ecosystem, all of them relying on each other, and when left alone, they do just fine. Humans tend to screw this up, but I am not going to address that here.

Our farm had the ten-acre woodlot mentioned above as part of it, which was contiguous with our farmland. Our woodlot was surrounded by other woods attached together by hundreds of official land deeds. The entire mountain was a mosaic of wooded parcels. They had been, and in many cases continue to be, owned by village residents, providing a source of firewood for their homes. The deeds for these woodlots were horribly written, and in essence, most of them are landlocked with no legal access. There must have been hundreds of verbal agreements allowing the crossing of the land of other owners.

I have always had a fond affinity for the woods. It is, in essence, a sanctuary of quiet. On days when there was only a light wind, the only sound I would hear was of a branch rubbing against another like an out-of-tune cello or a pileated woodpecker hammering its beak into a tree trunk for an elusive grub. If I was paying attention to where I was and turned my cell phone off in the woods, there could be no connection with the outside world. In the woods, there would be no phone calls or texts, no computer screen, no Facebook, and no bad Yelp reviews. One could be at peace with nature. It could be the perfect yoga studio if you were so inclined.

There are some minor drawbacks to having easy access to total solitude. If I needed a 2x4 or a hospital, it would be thirty minutes away. If I wanted to try on an LL Bean chore jacket or a new sports coat at Macy's, I figure it would be an hour's drive. But the cool part about where we lived (remember I am thinking about how close we were to the woods) was that we could leave our house and be standing in Times Square, the epicenter of a nine-million-person city, in ninety minutes. So, in essence, we can be transported from solitude to eye-popping digital mania before your first coffee break of the day.

If you have the opportunity and the funds to buy a piece of the woods, your choice will be rewarded in more ways than you can imagine. You may not have a "railroad" passing through it, but all the joys of nature will greet you every time you set foot in it.

THIRTY-SIX

Living With Wildlife

Many of the non-domestic creatures that reside on the farm are sometimes a source of enjoyment and, other times, a cause for consternation.

THERE IS QUITE A LENGTHY LIST OF ANIMALS LIVING IN THE State of New York. Most of them resided at or visited Glorie Farms during our farm tenure. Exceptions include a few venomous snakes, porcupines, beavers, and black bears. Copperheads and rattlesnakes do live in our county, but I have yet to make their acquaintance, and I am willing to wait. Some years ago, a nearby farmer friend needed to visit his veterinarian to have porcupine quills removed from his dog's muzzle, but none of these prickly creatures have been seen here. Beavers live just a half mile from our farm, but there are no ponds or streams for them to inhabit on our property. A bear was shot during the annual hunting season but was never shown to me. Bird species are mostly too numerous to mention, and we had no fish as we had no bodies of water.

We did, however, see everybody else from time to time. White-tailed deer and woodchucks were the most invasive. In any one season, there were likely twenty-five woodchuck families, also known as groundhogs, living on the farm. Their burrows wreaked havoc on hillside navigation when driving over bermed soil mined from the earth. These unpredictable mounds of earth can easily change the center of gravity and cause a tractor to flip over. Too often, stories have reached me about incidents that frequently didn't end well. These master miners were particularly fond of setting up quarters around our garden perimeter. I would classically trap five to ten per summer.

The deer were relentless. Our fifty-four-acre farm would be considered small, but on any one day, we could often count ten deer feeding on apple buds in the heart of winter. Neighboring larger farms could have a hundred deer visit in any one night. The newer planting systems create trees that are only twelve feet tall for easy harvesting. A deer can easily browse to five feet and higher if they decide to stand on their hind legs. Trees can be stripped of fifty percent of their fruiting wood over the course of a winter. Once a bud is removed, no apple will form in the coming spring, and hence, no fruit will be harvested in the fall. Apple buds form only once per season, unlike a tomato plant, which will form a new flower on a new shoot in the same summer.

I have applied numerous deterrents to the fruit trees with no effect. These include hanging bags of human hair stuffed into nylon stockings, mothballs, soap, Milorganite (dried human waste), and Bounce sheets. None of these work! There are, however, two solutions that do work. One is high-speed lead, as used in a 30-30 or 270 rifle. The best way to exclude deer is to construct an eight-foot-high steel fence around the perimeter of the farm. We waited thirty-seven years but finally erected a fence around forty of our acres. This approach is foolproof as long as the access gates are closed. If a gate is mistakenly left open, the deer will find the opening and enter. I swear there must be deer assigned to scout the fence line each night.

There was a period when we kept a cat or two in our barn to help deter mice. Of course, they could not live on mice alone, so we kept a small drum of dry cat food in the barn for their daily ration. This became a constant target for raccoons, woodchucks, opossums, and skunks. I likely captured fifty of these raiders over time. They were transported and released down the road near some other unsuspecting farm.

Birds were particularly pesky. They were quite fond of peaches, especially the crows. They knew exactly when to beak into a peach, which is always just when we want to harvest it. I know of no way to deter them. Our aviary natives are also exceptionally fond of wine grapes. We could always predict the first peck when the fruit reached twelve degrees brix. Brix is a measure of sugar content; an increasing brix number implies a higher sugar content. Birds can't be fenced out, but modest success was attained with the application of netting. We tried LP gas cannons, but a neighbor bitched about the noise. And he was one of our friendly neighbors and frequented our winery often. More about the winery later. The cannons make a lot of noise; some people are tolerant of the ballistics for the sake of a farmer's success, and others aren't. Balloons, shiny tape, and birds-in-distress recordings have all been tried with limited success. The newest deterrent is the use of laser light, which we never got around to trying. There were some harvest seasons when the bird attacks were relentless and other seasons when we saw no birds. I have no idea why this happened, but I never complained when they did not show up.

At one time, I found a muskrat cowering beneath the pickup truck. This was highly unusual as we had no bodies of water on or near the farm. These creatures are only found in small ponds and swamp environments. It was acting with some aggression, and I quickly determined it was rabid. I fetched my 22 rifle and ended it there.

Squirrel populations vary considerably from one year to the

next. The harvest season of 2020 brought unprecedented attacks on wine grapes by birds, raccoons, and especially squirrels. I witnessed a constant parade of them darting to and from the vines, from sunrise to sunset, mouths loaded up with berries, heading back to the woods.

Over time, one of our metal storage buildings was targeted by the squirrels. One side of the structure was open, and the rodents would come and go and did no damage. The other side had doors which, when closed, could exclude them. We got a little sloppy at one point and neglected to close the doors regularly. This was where Murphy stepped in. For those of you who are not familiar, there is a saying commonly referred to as Murphy's Law: "Anything that can go wrong will go wrong."

This storage area housed wine capsules, plastic wrap, and cardboard boxes, among other things. I arrived one morning to find the results of what must have been the squirrels' New Year's Eve party. There were piles of cardboard box litter, chewed wine capsules, and plastic wrap chards everywhere. The highlight of their escapades was their attack on the Kubota RTV, a Rough Terrain Vehicle. For some reason, squirrels are attracted to vehicle electric wires. It has to do with an odor the wires give off. I thought I could smell some alcohol from the champagne they were spilling about. At any rate, I had to call for Kubota service to do the rewiring. What address do I send the $700 bill to?

Raccoons not only frequented the vineyard but developed an affinity for our garden-grown sweet corn. Fences do no good as they can easily scale any height. Raccoons are nocturnal, so all the raiding was done at night. They possess a keen sense as to when to make the pick, which was always just before the ear was ripe. I had made three staggered corn plantings to extend the season, and they devoured every ear.

Foxes were a welcome addition as they could be useful in suppressing the vole population. Voles are mouse-like rodents that will girdle apple trees in winter under a protective deposit of snow. Well, I need to backtrack my praise a little as the fox kits loved to teethe on irrigation tubing, creating an array of small geysers rising from the orchard floor.

One summer, we were entertained by a young family of five foxes. Each night at dusk, we had the pleasure of observing their playtime just below our house deck. One morning, they did one better. We had fenced in the backyard to keep our chocolate Labs from wandering. The yard was filled with dog toys. I happened to look out at dawn one morning and found that I was a witness to morning playtime. All five kits were in the yard, each one with a dog toy in its mouth. It was hilarious to watch them scurry about, occasionally exchanging toys with each other.

Turkeys were nonexistent here forty years ago. The state did a good job of reintroducing them back into the wild. They flourished, and the local population once again became quite robust. We would commonly see flocks of thirty, and their visits were not always welcome. If we had to let grapes hang on the vine late into the season, seeking one more brix, we were often challenged by berry losses to turkey beaks. Many grape harvests were decided by how much loss we could tolerate before making the harvest call.

Our favorite visitor was and still is the red-tailed hawk. For many years, they would give us the special gift of nesting on the farm. These are truly a grand species of raptors. We rarely saw more than two at a time; they could have been a mom and dad pair or a mom and a fledgling. They would effortlessly glide on thermals, making 1,000-foot circles over the farm. In rare circumstances, we might witness an attack on some unsuspecting rabbit, snake, or field mouse, which provided sustenance for them for a couple days.

There was a one-of-a-kind event that occurred just prior to the grape harvest. It was one of those high-bird-pressure years. The farm staff had placed bird exclusion netting over the Cabernet

Franc vineyard rows. The work shift had concluded for the day, and they did not have enough time to clip the net in place. I had gone up to the vineyard to see how things were progressing. Soon after arriving, I noticed one of the nets dangling from an adjacent seventy-foot hickory nut tree. One end of the net was high in the tree, the other still lying on part of a row. My mind was tripping along, trying to figure out what had happened. Was it possible that a dust devil had come along to lift the net? A dust devil is a small swirling movement of air in an upward direction. That explanation was unlikely, so I concluded that a hawk had landed on the newly placed net, had gotten its claws tangled in the mesh, and in its attempt to exit the vine, took the net along, which then got deposited high into the tree. The hawk was long gone, leaving no other forensic evidence.

The presence of hawks in flight over a vineyard is a good thing. Birds are usually not a prime target for hawks, but they can be fair game in some circumstances. Birds expecting to feast on grapes will think twice about snatching a berry if they see a circling hawk or its shadow or hear its screeching call. I always felt a little better during the harvest season when I would see our raptor friend circling about high in the sky. It was like having a free bird deterrent program.

Several years ago, I got the idea that perhaps I could move the natural bird deterrent program along a little faster. I did some research on American Kestrels. Our native grape thieves are also fearful of Kestrels. I learned that these small raptors, members of the Falcon family, visited here in the warmer months. I confirmed this with our local DEC (Department of Environmental Conservation). Armed with this knowledge, while recuperating from a broken rib incident late one winter, I constructed a kestrel house with plans from the USDA. I erected the house on a February day in 2017 and waited. It is now 2021, and I am still waiting. But I have great news! This past spring, we were treated to the arrival of three American Kestrels. They still did not inhabit the house and must have decided on a hollow tree. We weren't fussy, and we're glad for their visit. We quickly fetched our binoculars and raptor handbook and figured out that we had one female and two males. We named the female Lizzy and the males Leo and Leo; we couldn't tell the males apart. We were entertained by their presence nearly every day until late August, which must have signaled the time to return to their winter quarters, which could be anywhere from Kentucky to New Mexico.

Of all the animals that have visited our old farm and now our retirement farm, the raptors are my favorite. And of all the raptors, I put the red-tailed hawk at the top of the list. It's a treat when I see one gliding back and forth over our farm, often never flapping a wing on a good thermal day. Sunny days will always create warm air currents to rise from the earth's surface. The hawks find these thermals and ride them up into the sky.

Our retirement farm, AKA Fourth Quarter Farm, seems to be a magnet for birds of prey. During spring and early summer, we have seen a short-eared owl, one Cooper's Hawk, one northern goshawk, one bald eagle, numerous turkey vultures (wow, are these ugly!), and, of course, Lizzy and Leos.

Paradise keeps getting better!

THIRTY-SEVEN

Don't Look Away

*Getting farm tasks accomplished at the right time
can have a positive effect on the bottom line.*

SUCCESS IN AGRICULTURE IS CLEARLY LINKED TO TIMING. Most farms follow a twelve-month calendar, and certain tasks or processes need to be performed at critical intervals in the annual sequence. A northeastern hay farmer knows that the ideal time to sow a new field of orchard grass is mid-August into mid-September. Planting earlier, he risks hot, dry conditions and likely poor seed germination and growth. Planting too late, when it is cooler, would produce a similar unsatisfactory result. Soil temperatures of seventy degrees are about ideal. One must pay close attention to the calendar and conditions on a daily basis and not look away.

Attention to detail is critical in all kinds of farming, regardless of the commodity being grown or the location of the farm. Sheep farmers in northern Scotland need to make the appropriate arrangements for the fall breeding season. Ewes must be herded back to the home farm, where the mating process can be monitored. Rams need to be inspected for health and vitality. New rams may need to be purchased for herd improvement. Sloppy planning could have negative results.

An ocean farmer operates under similar constraints. I recently read the book *Eat Like a Fish* by Bren Smith, where he enlightens the reader about farming seaweed, more specifically, kelp. Think of kelp as a sea vegetable. Kelp is also used as animal feed and agricultural fertilizer, and it is potentially a biofuel. East Coast kelp is considered a winter crop. Timing of the spore seeding is critical as the water temperature must be between forty-eight and fifty-six degrees Fahrenheit. Too early, the seed will be smothered by other seaweed. Too cold, the kelp can't soak up enough nutrients to get through winter.

Timing was so important for our farm that I produced an annual bar chart listing all the critical tasks, tracking each one weekly to be sure nothing was missed. We grew apples, pears, peaches, plums, raspberries, quince, currants, and wine grapes. For me, it was best to be tuned into the plants' phenology. Phenology is the study of periodic events in biological life cycles. In other words, what stage of growth is the tree in right now? Is it dormant, in bud swell, or in bloom, etc. Different tasks were performed at each stage of a plant's cycle. Our situation was somewhat unique because we grew numerous kinds of plants, all with different phenologies; tasks would constantly overlap each other.

Winter was dominated by the trimming of apple and pear trees. Trees and vines were pruned annually to maintain shape and vigor. The process could be initiated once the plants' wood hardened off, but starting too soon could coax late shoot growth only to be damaged by winter freezes.

Grapevines can be trimmed once their wood lignifies. This signifies that the plant material has become woody and is ready for winter. In the northeast, the process needs to be completed before May 5 as bud break is just beginning by then. Once the new bud begins to grow, it is highly prone to breakage and detachment from the vine. We wanted to keep as many buds as possible as these become flowers and, soon after, fruit clusters and the new year's crop.

Plant nutrients need to be applied three weeks prior to bloom; soil tests will have been done earlier to flag any deficiencies. Time is needed for spring rains to drive critical nutrient elements into the root zone. We wanted to have these elements in place before the bloom, as this period demands the most from a tree or vine. If our timing was off, the plant would not perform as well as it should.

The planting of new trees is done from late April to early May. Nurseries send out a farm's tree order to time their arrival in mid-April. Once the bare-rooted, still dormant trees arrive, they are placed into a thirty-two-degree cooler until planting conditions are optimal. For us, wet field conditions were usually the reason for delayed planting, but if we waited too long, the trees' buds would burst and flower in the cooler, and we would lose valuable growing time in the soil.

Other key sequential tasks include raking trimmings out from under trees and vines, chopping the trimmings, tying grape shoots to their support wires, mowing vineyards and orchards, thinning and positioning grape shoots, hand thinning excess fruit from the trees, managing weeds, applying crop protectants as scouting dictates, and installing bird control nets on the grapevines. Every event must be addressed during a critical interval of time. Tackling a task too late always results in profit hemorrhaging.

Harvest season is the king of events. The timing of the pick is no less important than all the other tasks. Determining the optimum time to pluck a peach was always a challenge. I have spent years trying to choose the perfect words to deliver countless descriptions to our harvest crew. A single peach tree would get picked three to four times. All the tree's fruit did not get picked in one pass. Even from tree to tree, the ripening speed can vary.

Doug Glorie

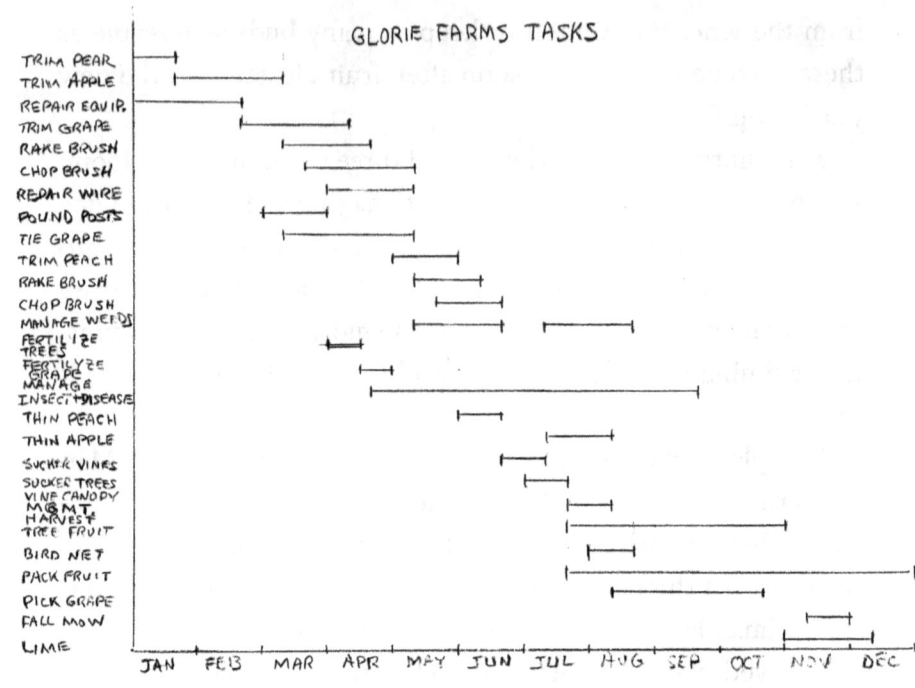

Farm task bar graph

The top of an orchard, at a slightly higher elevation, would ripen sooner than the bottom.

Peach tree varieties have been developed over time to spread out their fruit ripening dates during the summer months. We had staggered the variety planting on the farm so that we could pick and sell peaches over a seven-week period. Once the season commenced, we picked peaches every other day. The perfect window to pick a peach with optimum characteristics is two days wide. If picked too soon, a peach will lack flavor, color, size, and sweetness. If picked too late, it can be too soft and not ship well. Soft and dented fruit were culled from the picking lugs and destined for the compost pile, taking with them the profit that could have been.

Essentially, everything must go right on a farm for it to be sustainable. Timely execution is best not ignored.

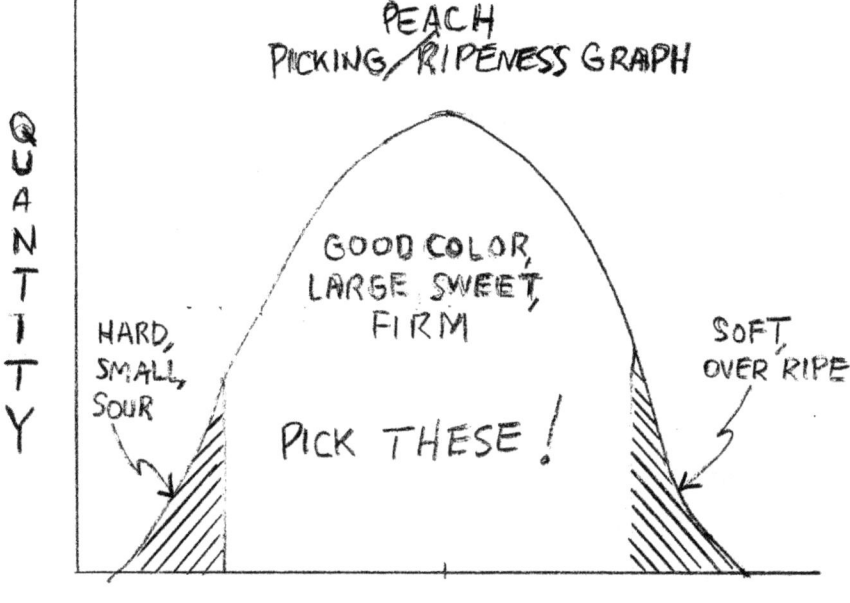

Ideal peach pick graph

THIRTY-EIGHT

Diversification

Growing multiple types of farm crops probably makes more sense than growing just one. I make my case.

IF I HAD IMPLEMENTED A COMPLETE DIVERSIfiCATION PLAN on our farm, it would have included peaches, nectarines, plums, apricots, cherries, strawberries, raspberries, blackberries, currants, quince, apples, pears, tomatoes, melons, garlic, mushrooms, grapes, Christmas trees, and beef cattle. I have grown all the above except garlic and mushrooms, and I have managed most of these crops at the same time. To be more precise, I managed about seventy-five percent of these crops at any one time. Crop selections came and went for various reasons. The question arose, Does this strategy make sense? Can a farmer successfully manage multiple plant, tree, and animal products at the same time? Producing all these items at the same time would, however, fulfill the desire to be fully diversified.

Another strategy could be the production of a monocrop, perhaps just one genus. It might make good sense to focus on just apples or only wine grapes. Both approaches have their pros and cons. My product decisions were easy at the beginning of my ag career. I had a full-time job with IBM, and when you do the math, I was off the farm for fifty hours a week. The best product fit in those years was pork, beef, pumpkins, and Christmas trees. These offerings did not require my undivided attention and allowed me to make a living off the farm.

This is a good place for me to flesh out my business case for propagating Christmas trees. As I alluded to in the previous paragraph, growing Christmas trees required little weekly attention and thus fit in well with my day job. There seemed to be a market for "cut your own" trees as others were already doing it. I began planting my trees in 1980, choosing the blue spruce as my sole variety because the deer wouldn't bother them. Their rigid, sharp needles were simply not mouth-friendly. The tree's annual care was not too intense but did require several grass mowings, one precisely timed May spray to ward off the leader borer, and as the tree matured, some trimming was done to produce the classic cone shape. The trees were purchased as ten-inch seedlings and cost less than forty cents a piece. Within a couple of years, I had 1,200 trees planted. Ten years later, I was able to begin selling eight-foot-tall trees at a price of $35 each. Of course, our personal tree was not permitted to be perfect (we sold those at full price) and always ended up being a Charlie Brown selection. By the early 2000s, MaryEllen was getting a bit tired of me being parked in the tree lot for the four weekends preceding Christmas, especially since December is her birthday month, so we decided to discontinue this venture.

I can make a case for both mono- and multi-crop choices, but I have always favored the diversified approach. There are a few large farms in our area—the Hudson River Valley—that only grow apples. The advantages are that the farmer will only need one type of equipment to service his orchards and will be dealing with a defined, limited set of insects and diseases to mitigate. His labor pool will be highly skilled at propagating and harvesting one crop. His markets are narrow and quite well-defined.

I have always felt that there is too much risk in choosing the monocrop avenue. A farmer can experience serious price swings from one season to the next when selling into a mono-crop market stream. There was a serious apple market crash in the '90s when Washington State experienced a bumper crop. The east coast apple market was returning $7.00 per bushel. Washington was sending Red Delicious 3,000 miles to our markets at $3.00 per bushel. Apples are a commodity, and Hudson Valley farmers had no choice but to lower their prices. The $3.00 price was well below the cost to produce them. Apple prices tended to stay suppressed for several years, causing some area farms to go out of business. If the apple farmer was also able to raise fifty head of Black Angus beef cows and ten acres of cut-your-own Christmas trees, the sting of poor apple prices could have been softened. We were fortunate during this period as we didn't have many apple trees, and we sold directly to stores, thereby avoiding the brokered market system.

In the early 80s, I had the opportunity to decide how to move the farm forward. I felt then, as I do now, that a diversified approach was the best strategy. Our main products then were the aforementioned pork, beef, pumpkins, and Christmas trees. I decided that the tree fruit and wine grape business was the direction to go in. I met with our county extension agent and set in place a plan to grow apples, peaches, pears, plums, and wine grapes. As the years progressed, quince, currants, strawberries, and raspberries were added. We tried apricots for a while, but they were a bit too cold-sensitive. Peaches became our queen crop and, at one point, covered half the farm. Peaches became our calling card, enabling us to access many stores, and then all of our other products could follow. The pork and beef were slowly phased out to the more profitable—and in some ways less aggravating—fruit

Me drilling post

business. Christmas trees gave way to wine grapes, and I didn't miss those twenty-degree December days trying to peddle those spiny blue spruce.

As with any great idea, it can be taken to an extreme. The diversification theme does have a few drawbacks; for example, different labor skills are required for each crop. The harvest criteria for a peach are completely different than for a raspberry. Each genus of fruit brought with it a unique set of insects and diseases. Finding successful control options was a continuous challenge as the parade of insects was relentless. I became an expert on wooly apple aphid, pear psylla, oblique banded leafroller, European red mite, and dogwood borer. I became intimate with all bugs' life cycles and the weather conditions in which they best flourished. Another complete set of knowledge was summoned to manage plant fungi, mildew, and viruses. As I write this, I am thinking how much easier it would have been to cover the farm in a mono-crop of Christmas trees.

Crop ripening schedules can also cause some stress when considering the diversified approach. The season started off quietly with strawberries in June, followed by raspberries by the fourth of July, and then peaches by week three in July. Plums followed in August, with apples, pears, and wine grapes in September. September was the most challenging month, as many of the crops' harvest weeks overlapped.

Over time, we had to make some cuts. Raspberries had to be picked every other day. They had a summer season (floricane) and a fall season (primocane), with each season lasting about three weeks. The typical summer season raspberry harvest day began at 7 a.m. and ended at 2 p.m. with the fruit boxed and loaded for delivery. One and often two trucks were sent out with the load and returned by 4 p.m. Essentially, every other day consumed twenty to thirty man-hours at the expense of the other crops. We eventually had to let the raspberries fade in favor of more lucrative and labor-efficient crops. Very early on, strawberries were dismissed. Too much disease and too close to the ground. We planted them once, and as MaryEllen placed the last few plants on her knees and supported herself on her elbows with her lower back screaming at her to stop, she said to me, "Please don't make me do this again." Next to go were the tomatoes. Simply too much competition with weak prices. Last to go were the plums due to their erratic annual cropping.

Sometimes, diversification can be a downright bad decision. In the mid-90s, we thought it would be wise to diversify beyond our farm boundaries. There was a nearby juice plant specializing in the production of apple cider. One of the partners wanted to sell his shares. We did our due diligence (which we can now report was clearly inadequate) and jumped aboard. Our cider was first class. Every jug was squeezed from at least three apple varieties, yielding a cider with awesome flavor. We were making inroads until we collided with a large competitor from an adjoining state. They were able to undercut our price and do it long enough to extinguish our company. We lost our entire investment. Lesson learned. And it was then that we decided the only partners we'd ever have in business were Doug and MaryEllen. Our accountant reminded us that partners are for dancing.

Our largest foray into diversification was establishing a winery, which began in 2001 and finally happened in 2004. That experience is a story in itself, which I'll cover in a separate chapter. For now, let's just say the idea pretty much came out of left field and caught us both very much by surprise. We had never considered a winery as part of our business plan. We did less due diligence for it than we had for the cider fiasco, so we did not know what we were signing up for. It's true that wine was our favorite adult beverage by then, but we knew little about how to create it and even less about how to sell it. Our ignorance was bliss, and we had a lot to learn, as you will see in a bit.

Taking on the winery was clearly an act of diversifying. Over time, it became nearly half of our annual income. In years when the farm suffered losses due to weather issues, the winery was there to soften the drop in income. It was not easy running the winery; we were saturated with work just operating the farm.

Adding the winery set a new standard for the term "hard work"; however, Glorie Farm Winery became the crown jewel of our enterprise. We initiated the sale of our farm and winery in 2019, and it was the winery that most people fell in love with. It was the best diversification decision we ever made.

THIRTY-NINE

Gravity is Your Friend

*Gravity is a natural force that
can enhance our daily lives.*

YOU QUITE LIKELY HAVE GIVEN LITTLE OR NO THOUGHT TO gravity since you first learned about it in the fourth grade. It is part of our daily lives and has existed on Earth since it was created. Sir Isaac Newton discovered the concept in 1665 when observing an apple falling from a tree. Being a farmer, I wonder what variety it was. Was it a Calville Blanc d'Hiver, France c.1500, or Pearmain, England c.1200, or maybe Melo D'Enzio, Italy c.450AD? I guess it is not important; from a gravity discovery point of view, an apple is an apple. We could not exist without this grounding phenomenon, pun intended, as we would float away to some distant galaxy. During my farming career, I have always tried to use gravity to my advantage. Most of us don't spend a microsecond thinking about the concept of gravity, but it could be viewed as useful if we choose to view it as such. Of course, there are numerous negative situations that one could reflect on, like falling in your driveway on an icy February day and landing on your ass or bumping your head on the blacktop and hoping no one was looking, but here I am going to consider the positive effects.

If you remember an earlier chapter, "The Art of Sledding," the fun my youthful friends and I experienced sliding down the snowy hill would not have been possible without gravity. If you enjoy skiing or snowboarding in the northeast, Colorado, or Utah, the thrill you experience sailing down a mountain slope on a cold, crisp January day could not be possible without gravity. And remember those trees I was cutting for firewood earlier? My chainsaw and I start the tree-felling process, but it is gravity that takes the tree down. Ever go to a water park in the middle of July when the thermometer registers 95°F and the humidity index is nearly the same? Getting to the bottom of the slide, feeling temporarily refreshed because of the cool water flowing over you, happens because of gravity.

Prior to 1960, most automobiles were sold with what's called a standard transmission. In order for the operator to reach cruising speed, one had to shift a manual transmission by depressing a floor-mounted clutch pedal while also maneuvering a shift lever through three and sometimes four gears to achieve highway speed. Many people reading this will have no idea how this is accomplished. Most cars manufactured after 1974 were produced with automatic transmissions, requiring no gear-shifting skills. I bring the clutch-shifted cars into focus because these models have an advantage should the operator experience a dead battery. If you know your car battery is dead or weak, you are unable to get a replacement quickly, and you need to be at work by 7 a.m. the next day, all you would need to do is first park your car on a hill overnight; setting the parking brake would be advisable. Then, in the morning, turn the ignition key to "on", depress the clutch pedal, place the transmission in second gear (first gear won't work; you will have to trust me as I have done this many times), release the parking brake, and allow the car to roll forward, complements of gravity, attain five to ten mph, then "pop" (release) the clutch and the car will start. You would not be able to do this with an automatic transmission or an electric car.

I often used this technique on the Hoeffner farm back in 1964 and on our farm during the last forty years. Nearly all farm tractors are equipped with manual transmissions. Assuming I knew the tractor's battery was weak or dead, and since we lived on a hillside farm, I would park the tractor on a hill and simply "pop" the clutch to start the engine. The "pop start" tactic preceded my Hoeffner days by over fifty years, as Henry Ford's Model T could be started with the same strategy. There is also an alternative procedure available if a farm has no hills; in this case, the "dead" tractor can be towed by another to replicate what gravity could have done.

I am still in regular communication with the new owners of our original Glorie Farms. They have since renamed it Nightingale Farm; the new owners are Dan and Jacqui Heavens. I help out from time to time at critical intervals and freely give advice, whether asked for or not. Even though we have no monetary relationship with Nightingale Farm, I still experience a sense of joy when things go well for them. As you know from previous chapters, the Glorie farm is a hillside farm that can be an asset when spring freezes occur. The month of May is a critical period for a fruit tree or grapevine. The trees and vines are producing flowers and tender fruitlets, which have essentially no tolerance for the number 32 on a Fahrenheit thermometer.

On the morning of May 18, 2023, between the hours of 5 and 7 a.m., the Hudson Valley experienced a freeze event. There was no wind during those early morning hours. Gravity plays a decisive role in a morning such as this one. Cold air is heavier than warm air, and as such, it falls off hillsides, collecting in the lowest spot it can find, like a valley or land depression. Most farms located in these cold-prone areas have installed wind machines for mornings such as this. Think of a wind machine as a gigantic immersion blender, mixing acres of air into a safe thirty-three-degree cocktail. On that still morning, the air in the valley just above the earth's surface was twenty-nine degrees, but thirty feet above the earth was likely thirty-five degrees Fahrenheit. As mentioned in an earlier chapter, a valley farm's investment in wind machines is essential to mitigate a freeze event.

Nightingale Farm experienced no cold-damaged fruit because gravity was their friend. The cold air simply fell off the mountainside farm, allowing the temperature to stay above thirty-two degrees, and I experienced one of the moments of joy; I think of myself as a cheerleader for their success.

I could go on with dozens of examples where gravity was used to make my farm life easier, and I will end with one more. On our retirement farm, AKA Fourth Quarter Farm, I needed to add drip irrigation to an evergreen tree planting in an area we nicknamed Blue Flats. Drip irrigation won't properly function with less than eight psi pressure. My water source is a spigot with 30 psi pressure, 150 feet away on the uphill side of Blue Flats. I know from my knowledge of physics that for every foot of elevation change in a downhill direction, I pick up 0.45 psi in pressure. The water is moved from the spigot to the trees via a ⅝ inch diameter hose. The bottom line is that even with pressure losses induced by the small hose and an in-line filter, gravity overcomes all of this, and I keep my needed eight psi minimum pressure.

Ok, I lied; one more thought, my drip example may be too complicated; after all, I am an engineer by degree, and I can get carried away. So, I will end with this, really. Have you ever participated in a soap box derby, either as a kid or as a parent helping your child? The Soap Box Derby became official in 1933. The race is made up of homemade cars built of orange crates, sheet tin, some scrap lumber, and baby-buggy wheels. They may be constructed with rudimentary brakes and usually steered by two ropes attached to the left and right sides of the front axle.

The course is set on a hill, and gravity does the rest. I built one when I was eight. I don't remember whether I used an orange or apple crate, but I know my wheels were re-purposed from a baby buggy. I never entered an official Derby race but spent many hours surging down our steep driveway. Just another instance of gravity being my friend. Now that I have sensitized you, I am sure you can come up with many examples where gravity is your friend, too.

FORTY

Birth of a Winery

*Two extra tons of grapes lead to
a new, unexpected business.*

WE NEVER INTENDED TO OPEN A WINERY. "WINERY OWNERS" was never something we aspired to become. We knew a lot about the taste of wine since we consumed it as if we were born in Bordeaux, France. As things happened, we were sort of pressed into it, pun intended. In 2001, our grape crop was huge. We spent several seeks harvesting the grapes, each cluster picked by hand, filling lug after lug after lug.

I had built a grape customer set over the years. Each year, we could lose a customer if someone died, moved away, or their doctor told them to cut back on wine consumption, but we would also add a customer or two so things balanced out.

BACK WHEN THINGS WERE SIMPLE

I need to do a flashback at this juncture to fill in a few details from the period 1983 to 2001. 1983 saw our first planting of grapes, which was the French hybrid Seyval Blanc, and its first commercial crop was in 1985. Our first customers for these grapes were some of the same people who purchased beef. These buyers were often semi-recent immigrants from Italy, Eastern Europe, or Portugal. They understood and spoke decent English but always with a heavy national accent. They often spoke to each other in my presence in their native language, which offended me somewhat. It was as though something was being hidden from me, but I never confronted them about it.

There was one customer who stood out, an Italian man named Joe. He was about five-foot-eight, fifty years old, and had a full head of hair going from gray to white. He was soft-spoken with a wonderful Italian accent, a friendly demeanor, and an easy smile, and I enjoyed doing business with him. He lived in Queens, Long Island, and had a wife and a couple of kids. He had been buying beef from us on an annual basis for several years. Each year, he would schedule a winter Saturday with me to come to the farm to slaughter his own beef cow. He would bring a couple of cousins along to assist with this job. When the grapes came into production, he would also come by one Saturday in September to pick up his allotment. We started a new tradition in the late eighties, which included lunch in our house after the beef slaughtering was done. Joe and family—males only—would take over our kitchen to cook salted cod, an Italian treat called Baccala. MaryEllen was not too fond of the lingering smell of salty fish, which seemed to cling to the kitchen air for days.

Once the fish was cooked, we would move downstairs to the cellar mud room to enjoy our meal in the warmth of the wood stove. Prosciutto, fermented green olives, baguettes of bread, and several bottles of homemade wine produced from the previous year's Glorie grapes rounded out the feast. It was like being in Sicily!

PLANTING MORE GRAPES

There came a time when having just white grapes was not satisfying our customers; they wanted red as well, and that led me to plant another French hybrid called DeChaunac in 1990. The wine grape business continued to flourish, creating the need for more plantings, which included additional Seyval Blanc, plus Noiret, Vidal Blanc, Cayuga White, and Cabernet Franc, all new to our farm.

I admit that the transition from growing beef cattle to adding grapes was not a smooth one. Rearing cattle was fairly simple: Supply some pasture, add hay, corn, and water, and the cows did the rest. A whole new skill set had to be learned for grapes, including knowledge of viticulture, entomology, plant pathology, and sprayer technology. Navigating issues of soil nutrient deficiencies, plus dealing with insects and diseases I never knew existed, was quite challenging. Applying crop protectants with an air blast sprayer was new territory for me as well. How fast do I travel down a row of grapes? What pressure should the pump be set at? What nozzle size should I use? Mistakes were made, and insects and diseases got ahead of me from time to time, but I eventually found a successful regimen.

2001—A WINE ODYSSEY

By 2001, the wine-growing business was doing quite well. At the end of harvest that year, we had satisfied all our customers' grape needs, but there was still a ton of Seyval Blanc (a white grape) and seven hundred pounds of DeChaunace (a red grape) hanging on the vines. We were not willing to settle for a loss of the remaining crop. I was well-acquainted with a nearby winery and one day, I paid them a visit. A woman named Anne was the winemaker and manager there at that time, and after a brief negotiation, we struck a barter deal. She would take our grapes and make wine for us. During the following year, she would get a half cord of firewood, a flat of raspberries, a half bushel of peaches, and a bushel of apples in trade for her enology skills. Anne was good at the bartering thing, and I credit her with my skill at it today. The resulting wine ended up filling four fifty-nine-gallon white oak barrels. Anne would later become our first winemaker at Glorie Farm Winery.

Over the next nine months, we patiently waited for the wine to age and morph into something wonderful. Of course, we occasionally tasted along the way to be sure it was heading in the right direction. The big day finally arrived the following spring, and when the bottling was done, we had 885 bottles of Seyval Blanc and 285 bottles of DeChaunac. Holy cow, now what!?!! We could not legally sell it, so we drank a bunch of it ourselves, of course, and also gave some to friends and relatives. The response surprised us when people tasted it and said, "This is delicious! Can we buy some?" I turned to MaryEllen and said, "They want to buy some. We should open a winery!" And that's when the seed for Glorie Farm Winery was planted. MaryEllen's initial reaction was less than jubilant; her enthusiasm for the idea didn't exactly match mine at the time, but we sparred a bit, and I kind of won her over. I can be very persuasive when I get excited about a new idea, especially when it's a new business venture.

There was additional motivation to enter the wine market. The farm can and has experienced some wild revenue swings primarily driven by weather events. We seemed to experience some type of hail event every year in our geographic area, and if it happened before fruit formed or after harvest, it had no effect. However, hail mostly forms during the hottest months when the fruit is well advanced but not yet picked, and it sits out in the open as a large target. The frozen rain pellets can be as tiny as BBs, as large as quarters, and anything in between. The damage can range from five percent of your crop to all of it in a matter of ten minutes. I might add here that I have found grapes to be relatively immune to hail because the berry wounds tended to heal over; plus, the poor appearance of a grape cluster is not important as they will get crushed into juice. The winery, a manufacturing business, would not be affected by adverse weather conditions, so it provided a safety net and a risk dilution to our composite business.

Once I convinced my accommodating wife to join me on this new adventure, I initiated the winery application process with state and federal agencies. It would take six months to establish a legal entity and longer to receive a winery permit. It was strongly recommended to us that we should engage legal assistance for the application process, but I'm a do-it-yourself and save-the-money kind of guy, so I spent numerous Saturday afternoons working my way through the applications one question at a time, calling the New York State Liquor Authority and the TTB to ask questions and get clarification as needed. When the application packets were as complete as I could make them, I enclosed the appropriate checks, put them in the mail, and crossed my fingers.

LOOKING FORWARD AND GETTING READY

Once our applications were submitted, the waiting period began. It would take several months for our applications to work their way through the evaluation processes, and during this time, we began preparing to open a winery. Even though we kept up with the French in wine consumption, we really lacked any detailed knowledge of winemaking, so we had homework to do. Terms like maceration, amelioration, and chaptalization were foreign to us. However, once the process started, we quickly learned what these new enology terms meant. Of course, we had no experience making wine, and we began to realize that the learning curve would be quite steep. Luckily for us, around this time, we learned that Anne would be leaving the local winery where she was employed. We met with her, and by the end of the meeting, we had hired our first winemaker.

I should pause for a moment before going on to the winery preparation process. MaryEllen agreed to start a winery based on the premise that our wine would be sold only to the wholesale market and that there would be no retail tasting room. This was a verbal agreement, with no handshake, nothing in writing, no contract, and I had my fingers crossed. I soon found that selling to the wholesale market was time-consuming, tested my patience, and was not highly profitable. I would often make an appointment with a restaurant or wine shop only to arrive and find out that the representative was unable to make it or forgot about the appointment. Meanwhile, I had taken three hours out of my farming day to no avail. Even when I made a sale, I realized that the profit margin was too thin to be sustainable. I had not thought these scenarios through carefully enough. It was at this juncture that I had to go back to MaryEllen and say, "We need to be able to sell our wine at the retail level, and we need to build a tasting room." Somehow, I was able to string enough positive phrases together, and she agreed. Little did we know how much this decision would affect our daily lives. MaryEllen and I had made numerous business decisions, most of them successful, so we moved forward with the winery plan feeling excited and confident.

The physical winery was produced by renovating our cattle run-in area beneath a section of our 1913 barn. I did all the work myself, having an adequate knowledge of carpentry. We visited a nearby supply house and quickly outfitted our winery with the basic equipment: a crusher/destemmer, bladder press, various stainless-steel tanks, and a wine pump. Soon after, we procured a bottler, filter/pump, corker, labeler, and capsular. In addition to these pieces of equipment, there was a long list of small items, i.e., corks, capsules, labels, test kits, etc., required as well. We quickly discovered when we were shopping for equipment to be used for processing beverages for human consumption, we could always double our estimated price for any one item. As the years went by, we learned there was no limit as to how much could be spent on equipment and associated tools. The need for equipment is never-ending. It took seven years to break even.

If nothing else, MaryEllen and I had a clear sense as to the type and style of wine made in other parts of the world. We had traveled to Spain, Portugal, Tuscany, France, and Canada, plus four trips to Sonoma, Napa, and the Russian River. I was going to include Ireland in this list, but remember that trip was for the Guinness. To educate ourselves about wine regions we had not visited, we just went to the town wine shop to get some samples. In producing wines at Glorie, we were driven by the sense of place. This is not a new concept and is referred to as "terroir." It is the integration of soil, climate, and geographic position where a particular wine is produced. Many wineries consider themselves unique, and we were of the same belief. Uniqueness can be expressed in many ways. A winery can differentiate its wines from others by growing a lesser-known grape variety, using a particular yeast, or aging wine for an extended period. We also believe that wine is made in the vineyard and hoped that the winemaker wouldn't screw it up. A combination of great vine management and sound horticultural practices will yield the happiest and most flavorful grape clusters. We simply wanted our wines to be authentic and express our unique positioning in the Hudson River Region. As such, we coined the tag line, "We grow Glorie wine." When you consider the journey from vine to bottle, the grape production portion is the most challenging. There are wineries in our region that grow their own grapes and make wine from them. In my opinion, these are the authentic wineries. I always took great pride in being one of these wineries. There are wineries that grow nothing and choose to buy grapes to make their wine, and that's okay. They may not have enough land to grow their own. There are wineries that buy bulk wine from other wineries, often from other regions. These are not authentic wineries. And then there are a few that buy finished, bottled wine from others. Are these really wineries?

DID THE HUDSON VALLEY NEED ANOTHER WINERY?

We never asked ourselves that question when we decided to jump into the wine business. If you recall a few paragraphs earlier, all we wanted to do was use up some extra unsold grapes. Spreading or diluting farm risks with the addition of a winery, essentially a manufacturing business, seemed like a sensible path to follow. We were also being swept along by the popularity of the New York State Craft Beverage movement. To be honest, we had no marketing plan. We simply made wine with what we had, Seyval, DeChaunac, and a Rosé (a blend of Seyval and a little bit of DeChaunac; we called it Rosanna Rosadannadanna). New York State had been known for its sweet wines, and that image has not entirely evaporated as yet. We are now number three among the wine-producing states and have made major inroads in the production of dry wines from grapes such as Riesling, Chardonnay, Cabernet Franc, Pinot Noir, and Merlot.

Glorie Farm Winery, the name we marketed our wines with, did have great success with producing and selling some sweet wines such as Candy Ass Red, Blackjack, and Rumple Pumpkin. It was hard to ignore the cash register ringing up sales with these wines. If I had to do it over again, I would produce only the classic dry Vinifera (French) wines like Chardonnay, Riesling, Pinot Noir, and Cabernet Franc. These grapes flourish in the Hudson

Valley, and wine connoisseurs recognize their names. More about Cabernet Franc will be discussed in the next chapter. As time went on, as it relates to the concept of having a marketing plan, one strategy stood out. It did not matter what style of wine we produced; it boiled down to the story behind the grape, why we decided to grow it, and, in many cases, how we named the wine. We learned that the story behind our farm journey, about the grape and, in some cases, the name on the wine bottle, was a bigger selling point than what was in the bottle. The story often made the sale. Did the Hudson Valley need another winery? Yes, and we are happy to have done it!

MAKING BETTER WINES

I belong to a loosely bonded local organization called the Hudson Valley Wine and Grape Association. One of the more meaningful things the group did for several years was conduct blind "wine in process" tastings. Commercial winemakers, as well as novices, met four or five times during the winter months and brought their yet-to-be-bottled wines of a certain type; for example, November might be Chardonnays, December might be hybrid whites, January might be red vinifera. Each bottle was bagged and numbered for anonymity, and then everyone tasted them sequentially, saying nothing but making notes with thoughts, comments, compliments, and suggestions for how the wine might be improved. Categories of evaluation included color, aroma, taste, and finish (often called aftertaste by the uninitiated). We rated each wine on a scale of one to four, four being the best and one being flawed or basically horrible. Upon bottle reveal, the identity of the wine would become known, followed by the winemaker's specs and the processes followed to produce the wine. It could be intimidating and downright painful to hear the naked truth of your peers' reviews, but it worked because, additionally, experienced winemakers in the room offered suggestions for how to mitigate problems with the wine or identified techniques that might be utilized to improve next year's vintage. Over the course of the next several years, as a result of all this knowledge sharing, the quality of our Valley wines clearly improved. Sound, well-made, balanced wines were and are being vinified from Seyval Blanc, Chardonnay, Pinot Noir and Cabernet Franc. Many other varieties of vinifera and French hybrids are grown and vinified here as well. Nearly all of us send wines out to the many annual wine competitions conducted all over the country. These independent, blind ratings further guided winemakers as to how their wines were perceived and often resulted in garnering more medals.

TRIALS

An important aspect of making great wine is to perform bench trials. This is the process of regularly sampling cellar wines in progress. Small samples are thieved from tanks and barrels to sense how they are developing and to be sure there are no detectable flaws. The wine is viewed, swirled, sniffed, sipped, swooshed and spit. If I'm being honest, not all the wines were spit, so it could become a delightful afternoon.

Blending trials were more interesting and were MaryEllen's favorite part of the winemaking process. Wine is often improved when different barrels or tanks are blended. Another variation of blending is putting different varieties together. An example of a multi-century blend is the French wine of Bordeaux. Only French wine produced in the Bordeaux region can be called Bordeaux. Its blend classically contains Cabernet Sauvignon, Merlot, Cabernet Franc, and a few other grape varieties that are legal in small amounts. Other wine regions around the globe can blend the same varieties but cannot call the resulting wine Bordeaux. In our case at Glorie Winery, we produced a blend of the same Bordeaux varieties but called it Synergy. We described it simply as a "Bordeaux style." Blending trials in sequential vintages will rarely yield the same varietal proportions. One grape may shine brighter in any one year causing a blend shift.

Not all trials go smoothly. We made a blended wine we named Red Monkey. We had produced it from the beginning. The wine contained three grape varieties with percentages tweaked for each vintage. We conveyed to the winemaker a battery of blend considerations, and he/she configured a lineup for our tasting evaluation. For one vintage, we went through seven variations with no obvious leader. Our palates were getting fatigued, and we called it quits for the day. Our panel of tasters included me, MaryEllen, and the winemaker. We also occasionally invited wine connoisseurs and Glorie fans to round out the judgment. Our intent was always to release an awesome wine. We restarted our Monkey trial the next morning. MaryEllen suggested that we add two percent of a variety not used before, and presto bingo, it was a winner. Patience and perseverance paid off.

Occasionally, mistakes are made during the wine production process. Yes, we, as humans, make mistakes. Sometimes, we can say sorry and move on. But if you have just made a procedural error on 300 gallons of wine, a simple sorry won't fly. The batch may have a retail potential of $20,000. We need to step back and look for a save. One season, we were four months along on a peach wine, and tasting trials told us that the wine needed a little sweetening. No problem; this is routine; just back-sweeten with a little sugar. Anne made the calculation, indicating the need for five pounds of sugar. I weighed out the sugar and left it for Anne to add while I went off to do another task. A week later, I re-tasted the wine only to find a beverage more like lemonade than wine. I turned to Anne and asked, "What did you do to the wine?" She was without words. After backtracking my steps, I realized what had happened. Sugar had come packaged in brown bags, and citric acid had been in yellow bags. But a recent citric acid delivery came in brown bags. I had mistakenly added five pounds of citric acid, which more than explained the tartness.

Citric acid is a natural acid found in fruit like lemons and can be used in wine to brighten the "mouth feel." We needed to go into rescue mode, perhaps another Belted Bartletts-style creative solution. MaryEllen arrived home from work that day just as I was cleaning up the winery lab. I told her what had happened and that we needed a solution to save the wine, or we were going to lose a fair amount of money. She thought for a few minutes and then suggested that maybe we could add more wine to the batch to lessen the effect of the citric acid. We did a few trials of adding some of our Vidal Blanc to the bitter blend and tweaking the sweetness a little, and we had a winner. The new wine was even better than our original formula. We continued to make our Peach Wine that way every year thereafter.

TAXES AND FEES AND REPORTS, OH MY!

I suspect that people who are business owners have a different perspective about government than those who simply work for a business. Regulations, filings, fees, inspections, and business-specific taxes would often cause me to think bad things about our system. On the farming side of the business, we had to deal with the DEC (Department of Environmental Conservation), the DOT (Department of Transportation), plus New York State labor and compensation audits. Any deviation from the statute could result in a fine. I felt we were close enough to state and federal agencies by filing annual income tax for the farm, but now that we were selling alcohol, the reporting requirements rose exponentially.

Now, we had to collect sales tax, pay the excise tax, and report to the big guy, the TTB (Tax and Trade Bureau). Businesses such as wineries, distilleries, cideries, and breweries that deal with alcohol enter a new arena of scrutiny and taxation. My blood pressure always rose when we wrote the annual $200 check to New York State just to satisfy the requirement to tell them we were still in business at the same address. And then, there was the $25 fee to e-file our signature to the state. These fees and filings are relentless and grow in number and dollars every year, and yet these have nothing to do with making and selling alcohol. But I digress....

TTB is a federal agency whose main goal is to be sure every gallon of all alcoholic beverages produced is documented—a holdover from Prohibition—and that the excise tax on it gets properly identified and paid. It was during the Prohibition era that organized crime produced, distributed, and sold volumes of tax-free booze, a practice known as bootlegging. I have been told that there is a two-inch-thick book defining the TTB rules governing the production of wine, beer, and spirits. Obviously, it's impossible to know all the rules, which I suspect might be intentional. The best a winery can do is to not raise any TTB flags. If TTB agents should visit your winery, it will be unannounced, and you might as well hand over your checkbook because they will find a violation, and you will be fined. We were lucky and never saw an agent.

The scariest time of the year for me was the period from January 1 to 15. All U.S. wineries must file a Report of Wine Premises annually by January 15. My ass tightened, and my blood pressure spiked at the thought of preparing the filing. I likened it to getting a tooth pulled without anesthesia, having hemorrhoids removed, or being served divorce papers. The harmless-looking form covers a single, two-sided sheet of legal-length paper. It appears to be straight forward, but the devil truly is in the details, as they say, and each line can lend itself to misinterpretation.

"What do they really want me to enter here?" We made every effort to keep accurate records of each step in the winemaking process for all of our wines. Theoretically, this can make the form completion an easy process and facilitate a smooth filing, but it has never happened. The form's math check is very simple. Line 4 must equal line 18. One starts with gallons ending the previous year, new wine is fermented, and there are some losses to bottling and evaporation (also called the "angels' share"). Our lines 4 and 18 NEVER once matched, and I made my call to Sherlock. Now, I would go into frenzy mode. I poured over our records in an attempt to find an error or omission. This worked some of the time, but too often, I needed to engage my creative gene. There is a line called "losses." Then I remembered the faulty tank valve which leaked wine. How much did it leak? Answer: enough to get line 4 closer to 18 while not flagging TTB. Then, there was a line called "family use." This was my go-to line. There was no hard and fast rule that clarified just how much wine could be entered here. I always tried to put myself in an auditor's shoes and come up with a plausible number. Needless to say, the "family use" line could vary from year to year to satisfy the ledger balance.

At this point, you might wonder how a winery that started with two over-produced grape varieties got to be a two-thousand-case facility. It does not magically happen, and it would be very difficult with just two wines. We knew very early on that we needed to diversify. We were trying to make the wines that we liked, those being bone dry. But many people drink sweet wines, and we were missing out on these potential sales. We were also making wine with unfamiliar varieties that were hard to pronounce. Our wine visitors could easily identify with Cabernet, Riesling, and Chardonnay, so we embarked on a multi-year planting program. Along the way, we had to sacrifice some pear and peach trees. There was some open land on the farm, but I was challenged to manage what we had. Then there was the rule that MaryEllen laid down a few years prior, "You have all you can handle on your plate, so if you want to plant something new, you'll need to take something out." Divorce was not an option, so I complied!

We listened to our customers and took trips to the Finger Lakes region, as they were a little ahead of us in the diversity aspect. We quickly added semi-dry pear, apple, and the aforementioned peach wines. We were already growing these fruits for the fresh market, so there was ample raw material from natural cullage.

We also paid attention to trends. Rosé was popular in the mid-2000s, so we simply blended a little red DeChaunac into our Seyval Blanc, and presto bingo, we had Rosé. We came across a pumpkin wine at a winery in Massachusetts and decided we could duplicate its flavor, so we did, and it became our top seller. We kept uncovering new flavor profiles that customers embraced. We knew our customers' palates and had gathered enough experience to know when a new wine would be successful before making it. We added blackberry, black currant, and late-harvest wines, each one gathering a following. We also brought on Cabernet Franc, Riesling, and Chardonnay for our dry wine customers. Sometime around 2012, hard ciders were rising in popularity, so we produced a couple versions to move with the trend.

We added new wines, dropped less popular wines, played around with wines, opened a tasting room, won some medals, met a ton of people, made a little money, met some challenges, created some gin and brandy, drank a lot of wine, and generally had a good time. So, looking back, giving birth to a winery because we couldn't sell a couple tons of grapes turned out just fine.

Me in '58 Chevy

FORTY-ONE

A Coalition

A signature grape for the Hudson Valley.

In winery terms, a geographic area that produces wine in a state, or for that matter anywhere in the USA, gets an appellation designation. New York State has seven AVAs or American Viticultural Areas. The Glorie Winery is in Marlboro, NY, and, therefore, in the Hudson River Region appellation. It is the aspiration of most wineries to produce awesome wine, grow sales, and make more money. In my opinion, achieving this goal can be enhanced by having multiple wineries in a region rally around a common goal. New York is the third largest wine producer in the country. The state has seven very diverse growing regions that align with the AVA's. These regions compete against each other to some degree in getting potential wine customers' attention. The Hudson Valley is unique in that it is the closest AVA to the population prize of New York City. We needed to get on their radar by highlighting something special about our wine region. An attempt was made through the efforts of the Hudson Valley Wine and Grape Association in the early 2000s. As a unit, we agreed to make two blends unique to the valley and promote them. They were Hudson Heritage White and Hudson Heritage Red. The white featured Seyval Blanc, and the red featured DeChaunac because these two grapes grow well here, we had a decent amount of acreage, and they make solid wines. However, the concept did not flourish due to the lack of winery buy-in.

We make a vast array of wine styles in our valley. Another tactic to promote ourselves would have been to focus on our diversity, but it is hard to focus on a broad topic. Besides, if you ask a wine drinker to name their favorite style of wine, you'll never hear, "Oh, there's so much diversity in wine, and I love them all!" Realistically speaking, how do you highlight fifteen different styles at the same time? It's just too confusing. Each winery has a portfolio leader, which might be a dry red, a sweet white, a fruit wine, a sparkling, a pure varietal, or a blend. Most famous wine regions are known for a specific grape variety. Burgundy is Chardonnay, Tuscany is Sangiovese, Napa is Cabernet Sauvignon, and our New York Finger Lakes is Riesling. It seemed clear to me - and to many other people - if it was going to grow as a wine region, the Hudson Valley needed a signature grape.

During the period from 2013 to 2016, I was on a crusade to identify the Cabernet Franc grape and its wine as the Hudson Valley's leader. First, it has the name Cabernet in it, and everybody has heard of it. Nobody even knows what DeChaunac is, much less how to spell it. Cabernet Franc is made by many of our valley wineries, is the most planted grape in our region, and tastes as good as Loire Valley Francs, if not better. It is the natural fit for our signature grape, and the other AVAs around us wanted to claim it for their own. Let's get rolling! I felt the timing was right, and there was some momentum building. Steven Kolpan, a local wine guru, had written an article in Valley Table Magazine in 2014, also making a case for Cabernet Franc as the signature grape of the Hudson Valley. In parallel, during the same period,

MaryEllen was doing research with other New York State wine regions. Her research led her to the same conclusion, rally around one grape! We approached Linda Piero and Bob Bedford of the Hudson Valley Wine Magazine in early 2016 to see if they would buy into this concept, and with the support of many Hudson Valley wineries, we promptly formed the Hudson Valley Cabernet Franc Coalition, which is directed by Linda, Bob, MaryEllen and myself. Our focus is to call attention to the Cabernet Franc grape and its wine being made by our seven-member wineries, thereby establishing a Cabernet Franc brand identity for the Hudson River Region. We developed a wine standard to assure quality and consistency. Bottled wines meeting the standard can have a bottle seal of the coalition's black hawk logo displayed on the bottle. Look for it during your next visit to your favorite wine shop.

Hudson Valley logo

FORTY-TWO

Live Until Tomorrow

The phenomenon of mutation affects all of us.

I AM NOT CERTAIN THAT, TO THIS POINT IN THIS BOOK, I HAVE adequately sensitized you to the complexity of issues a farmer is confronted with and the knowledge he must possess to be successful. All farm tasks must be performed nearly perfectly to get to the annual finish line and claim a profit. A major natural phenomenon that challenges a farmer has to do with mutations of plant fungi and insects. We all now possess an understanding of what a mutation can become due to our exposure to continuous news reels covering Covid-19. Multiple variations have occurred since Covid-19 first arrived in early 2020, and keeping vaccinations effective has kept drug companies on their toes.

The concept of mutations is not new to a farmer. I'd like to preface this section by referring to a piece of knowledge I gleaned from the book *A Brief History of Nearly Everything* by Bill Bryson. He describes a common theme shared by one of the simplest forms of life, lichen—a tiny green fungus often found growing on rock, usually about three-eighths inch high, sometimes adorned with a tinier red flower—and the most complex, you and me, the humans. Both life forms have basically one goal: to live another day, to live until tomorrow. Hold this thought for a moment.

Each week, you or someone in your family visits a grocery store or market to pick up fresh fruits and vegetables. And yes, while you are there, you grab a bag of potato chips and a box of Cheerios. And sure, you will likely pick up some milk, eggs, and maybe a six-pack of Bud, but these are not part of my analogy. However, if there was a broken potato chip wafer or a half Cheeri "O," I'm fairly certain you would still eat it without hesitation.

But when you push your cart through the produce aisle and examine and choose an apple or peach, you will avoid and not pick up a piece of fruit with a scar from an insect bite or mildew tarnish on the fruit's surface. You only pick up the perfect, unblemished fruit. Do you know what it takes to produce the perfectly formed, clean-skinned red apple?

I'll use apple and grape production to enlighten you about what it takes to produce "clean" fruit. The apple production or growth cycle begins about April 15 when fruit buds are moving from dormant to green tip stage. As soon as the bud opens and green tissue is exposed, the apple scab pathogen is ready to strike. Scab spores overwinter on the orchard floor and are awakened by rainfall and warm temperatures in the spring. I will need to initiate my scab protection program now. I will scour my *Cornell Recommends* book to find what chemicals are useful in the prevention of scab. I will look for the one that has the highest efficacy rating at the lowest cost. Some will be considered "organic," but most are not. Ninety-eight percent of the "hard" chemicals are gone and have been banned, and this is good for you, me (as the person who handles and applies them), and the planet. The old chemicals were a broad spectrum, taking care of multiple issues with one chemical, and they were cheap. The new chemicals are "softer," highly selective (protects against one disease or insect), and expensive but better for the environment.

As the season progresses and temperatures rise, different disease pressures arise, and once an apple fruitlet forms, insect pressure goes up. At each spray interval (a tractor-driven air blast sprayer is used to apply the protectants), I drag out the Cornell book to choose the best protectant option. I will need to apply about twelve sprays during the growing season to ensure you get pretty fruit on the produce shelf. You might be thinking here, couldn't you be less diligent and stretch the application interval or skip a spray? And I have thought about this. So, let's say I am willing to accept an eight percent cull rate for scab blemishes, six percent for curculio marks, seven percent for apple maggot borings, and four percent for sawfly scores. Just these four defects remove twenty-four percent of my yield. At this rate, there would be no profit margin left, resulting in an unsustainable future for my farm.

You should be pleased to know that modern American farmers are continuously striving to reduce their reliance on chemical protectants. We want our soils to remain healthy and vibrant for centuries to come. I used organic materials when I was farming full-time and expect to use more of them in our new grape planting. And I am happy to share with you that a new regime of biologics is being offered. These new materials keep the plant healthier, enable it to ward off disease, and, in some cases, teach the plant to activate its own immune system—not unlike Moderna's mRNA delivery technique used in the Covid-19 vaccine. We have come a long way from using DDT.*

I am going to switch crops at this juncture to punctuate my point for this chapter. Viticulture—growing grapes—is slightly

---

* DDT, Dichlorodiphenyltrichloroethane, is an insecticide, developed in the 1940s and banned in the United States due to its toxicity to humans and wildlife in 1972. It is, however, used in some countries to control mosquitoes that spread malaria.

easier than growing apples because wine grapes don't have to have a completely clean appearance. After all, they just get crushed, pressed, and fermented, but they must be free of rot. However, ensuring grapes are free of fungus and rot in the Hudson Valley can be a challenge most years.

Many wine grape varieties are susceptible to powdery mildew, not just here but all over the world. If you live in a rural or urban area in the northeast and have lilacs planted on your property border or have propagated bee balm or zinnias, you know what powdery mildew is. It attacks the leaves, causing a reduction in photosynthesis and resulting in poor plant health. Keep in mind powdery mildew is only one of four major grape and vine pathogens that a farmer is confronted with each growing season.

In an agricultural environment, if the disease is visible on the grape leaf, it is already too late. The farmer must understand the life cycle of the disease and be cognizant of the favorable conditions for its growth before it can be seen. I know from experience that powdery mildew can strike as early as two-inch shoot growth. So, it's back to the Cornell book to choose a protectant for what will be spray number one. I choose a chemical based on its FRAC class, Fungicide Resistance Action Committee. Each class of chemicals will have a unique mode of action or MOD. Each class will interrupt a different sequence in the organism's life cycle. These new chemicals are not poisons; they are life cycle disruptors.

The same approach is applied to the development of modern insecticides. These materials could, for example, interrupt an insect's digestive process or reproductive system and have no adverse effect on our environment.

Each FRAC class must be used judiciously throughout the season so as not to "wear out" the chemical. Even though I may be happy with a chemical's performance and cost-effectiveness, I know that I cannot apply it on a sequential basis for fear of a fungus mutation. There will be nine more spray applications during the remainder of this growing season, mostly to do with powdery mildew prevention. I must be diligent with each spray and careful not to repeat a FRAC class. I know from both education and experience that the powdery mildew pathogen will reinvent itself and mutate around an overused protectant because all it wants to do is live another day. It just wants to live until tomorrow.

FORTY-THREE

Physics and Farming

*The science of physics and its application
can often be beneficial in a farm environment.*

I HAVE SPOKEN SEVERAL TIMES IN THIS BOOK ABOUT MY FAScination with the science of physics and how it was applied and observed on our farm. The science of biology also plays a large role and, to a lesser degree, that of chemistry. I don't profess to be much of a physics theorist, but I am adept at its application. Owning a farm has opened my mind to the many ways energy is produced and witnessed in a farm environment. Two theoretical forms of power come to mind. One has to do with Work, $P=W/T$. P is power, W is energy transferred, and T is the unit of time. The other form is the Watt, which equals one joule per second. Over the course of a calendar year, we would encounter a lengthy list of power and force that naturally occurred on our farm.

One form of power we frequently witnessed was that delivered in a lightning strike. Lightning is usually produced during a thunderstorm. These storms got our attention due to the magnitude of noise created, the spectacular light show displayed, and the visual and audible sound effects produced by the wind. If there was hail in the storm, the effect took on a new dimension in the form of damaged fruit and loss of income. Upon a storm passing, we would wonder, *Did we just experience a direct hit?* There was an occasion when we heard a "snap" followed by a power outage. A follow-up investigation at the breaker panel revealed the odor of burnt plastic and a damaged main circuit breaker. The breaker did its job by protecting the house but was destroyed by what was likely a voltage surge on the utility line. The breaker was replaced to serve another day.

So, back to my question, "Have we ever experienced a direct hit?" The answer is yes. I found an apple tree in the orchard south of the barn shortly after a storm, displaying the telltale signs of a direct strike. The tree had a continuous bark split, spiraling from top to bottom. A lightning bolt contains an enormous quantity of energy and heat, causing the water inside the tree to instantly boil and burst the tree bark.

Power outages would occur on average three times per year, caused by a downed tree or snapped electric pole on a road leading to the farm. Power restoration was usually completed within four hours; however, outages have lasted twenty-four to forty-eight hours, and during one winter event, it lasted for four days when there was widespread transmission wire damage. We invested in a whole-house generator in 2012 but could not justify a larger one for the farm, even though it was highly dependent on a continuous supply of electricity. A short-duration outage was of no consequence, but when it lingered into the double-digit hours during the middle of summer, the situation became serious. On any one day during the latter part of August, our two coolers were chock full of peaches and could be holding a quarter of the season's pick. It was during these events that I would hop into my pickup and try to locate the restoration crew to register my sense of urgency. And in all cases, just when I backed my trucks up to our cooler to load the palettes of warming fruit to be transported to a neighbor's cooler, the lights would come on, and all was well with the world.

We experienced four to five thunderstorms per year on the farm. Usually, two of them were violent enough to cook our irrigation system's control board. The board operated with a 24-volt DC system and was simply too wimpy to withstand any lightning-induced voltage surge, and it failed. I had tried several strategies to deflect the surge with no effect. I conferred with my friend Rob, who I respect as he has significant knowledge in the science of physics. He said I should try to lure a potential lightning strike away from our buildings, so I did. I located the tallest oak tree at the top of our mountain. I hauled my fifty-foot ladder up the hill and extended it to its maximum length against the tree. I stapled a quarter-inch diameter copper wire to the tree from top to bottom, terminating it to a ground rod at the base of the tree. In theory, the lightning should favor the elevated copper conduit and spare the irrigation wiring. I don't believe it had any effect, but at least I tried.

There are 1.5 billion lightning strikes per year around the globe. Each strike contains one billion joules of power. To say it another way, a single strike could, if harnessed, power a home for almost two weeks. Unfortunately, there is no way to capture this power as it occurs essentially instantaneously, and there is no equipment available to collect it. So, for my first example of harnessing the potential power of physics, I have led you down a dead-end path. Perhaps someone will design a way to capture the power of a lightning strike in the future.

We had success harnessing another source of power from the heavens. We've harvested photons from the sun. Between 2009 and 2014, we installed two solar arrays, which produced 25,000 watt-hours of electricity annually. It amounted to about seventy percent of our yearly needs. The systems would pay for themselves in ten and twelve years, respectively. As of this writing, both systems have paid for their investment costs and could be considered to be producing free electric power. We expect the production life of the systems to exceed twenty-five years.

Sometimes, my mind will take me on mini-physics journeys. Bear with me on this. I have felled many large trees in our woods over the past forty years, and I often think of the energy produced by their fall. The energy was produced by the mass of a tree falling to earth with the aid of gravity. After five seconds, and with the help of Newton's second law, the tip of the tree was moving in excess of 110 miles per hour. An oak tree with a girth of twenty inches and seventy feet tall has a significant mass. So, to demonstrate the energy produced in this tree's fall, picture this: Suppose I could place a large, very strong plank such that the tree tip would land on one end of the plank. I place a beefy barrel under the center of the plank, and I stand on the other end of the plank. I am six foot one and weigh 185 pounds. In my teeter-totter example, I am trying to paint a picture of the energy developed in the tree's fall. So, I cut the tree, run over to the other end of the plank, hop on, and wait about one second. How high will the impact of the tree landing on the opposite end of the plank send me? I suspect nearly seventy feet, the height of the tree just before it was felled. Wow, what a ride that could have been! Think about all the millions of trees felled each year and all the energy produced by each fall. If only there was a way to capture all this energy.

On a more practical note, if I took the same tree that just launched me seventy feet, cut, split, and dried it, I would have a meaningful source of energy to heat our house, which is exactly what I did for forty years. There are twenty-four million BTUs of heat in a cord of red oak. Four cords heated our house during the heating season. We likely saved $2,000 per season on our fuel oil bill.

Not all natural physics phenomena have to do with energy. The freezing of water can produce amazing pressures. Apple trees in late winter can be fooled by a warm day in March. Sunlight striking the south side of the trunk of a young tree can cause the tree to take on water into its vascular system. At night, if the temperature falls back into the twenties or teens, the water can't retreat fast enough back into the earth, and the residual water will freeze behind the bark. Water expands in volume when it freezes, which often causes the bark to expand and split. The split becomes an entry point for disease in the spring, but our partners at Cornell have taught us that applying white paint to the trunk on the south side can mitigate the issue by reflecting the sun's rays.

Anyone who has walked the woods in the Northeast has witnessed the power of freezing water. Multi-ton boulders of granite lie split open due to the force of ice expanding in the rock's fissures. Your automobile tire has 32 psi in it. I wonder how many psi it takes to split a granite rock.

There have been some high-pressure, natural events that have occurred in our winery. In order to have a successful winery, one must carefully follow a multi-step process to convert grape juice into alcohol. At one point, yeast is added to the juice, which converts the sugars in the juice into alcohol. The process is called fermentation. A major byproduct of this process is carbon dioxide gas. For red wine, the yeast is added, or in wine terms, "pitched" into the "must." Must is a mixture of juice and grape skins. In one particular instance, we had five fermentations going in one-ton plastic bins. Red wine produces a "cap" caused by all of the grape skins collecting on the surface of the must. The cap gets "punched" down twice a day to mix it with the juice below by thrusting a punch-down tool through the cap. On this morning, the first punch caught me completely off guard. I made my first plunge, piercing the cap, and was greeted by a must explosion. It was like a mini bomb went off. There was no audible bang, just grape skins and red juice landing everywhere, including me, nearby windows, and the electric panel. The eruption was due to a rapid production of carbon dioxide gas under the cap. The gas could not escape fast enough through the cap, and my piercing the cap was like popping a balloon. I later learned that the winemaker was experimenting with some new yeast strains. This choice was simply a bit too aggressive.

Here is another illustration of how much energy can be produced on a farm. Let's consider our former farm, for example. There were twenty usable acres for planting fruit. Let's assume I had all twenty acres planted in apples. Let's also assume that the acreage yielded 1,000 bushels per acre (assume a hundred apples per bushel), which is a reasonable yield for our region. Each apple harvested represented ninety-five food calories (energy). When I did the math, our farm had the capacity to generate 190,000,000 calories per year from 2,000,000 apples. That's a pretty good feeling!

The power generated by water in motion is enormous. In centuries past, much rural power was produced by placing a paddled wheel in the path of moving water as in a grist mill. Seven percent of 2021 US domestic electricity was produced by water flowing through a turbine, a high-tech re-configured paddle wheel.

I witnessed the fury and power of flooding water more than once on our old farm. The most recent was on Memorial Day some ten years ago. We experienced a four-inch rain event occurring over a one-hour interval. To put this into perspective, an inch of rain falling onto an acre of land equals 27,143 gallons. This one-hour rain event deposited nearly six million gallons of water onto our farm. Due to the natural topography of our farm, most of this water channeled to the driveway. In a matter of two hours, the bottom third of our driveway was washed away, and there was nothing I could do to stop it. Fifty tons of stone were moved from our driveway to an adjacent parcel across the street. We soon invested $12,000 in water diversion tactics, which appear to have resolved the issue thus far.

Earlier in this chapter, I told you about our farming photons. Suppose we could harvest rain. Suppose for one year, I could collect all of the rain that fell onto our fifty-four-acre farm and turn it into power. I could direct the water downhill to an eventual turbine and convert the flowing water into electricity. During the year 2021, an average of fifty-six inches of rain fell in New York State. So, in order for me to pull off this rain harvest plan, I would need to construct one very large basin or vessel, 4.67 feet tall, 800 feet wide, and 3,300 feet long (actual dimensions of our fifty-four-acre farm). The basin would hold 82,000,000 gallons of water. How much power could I generate? Would it be worth the investment?

I put together an analysis that goes like this. I need to move the eighty-two million gallons via a pipe to a turbine below our elevation. The flowing water would spin the turbine fins, which would spin a generator shaft and produce electricity. The turbine would be located on the Hudson River in Marlboro, three miles east of our farm. The elevation of Marlboro on the Hudson is about 155 feet above sea level. The average elevation of our farm is 700 feet. The difference is 545 feet. This number is called "head." Picture a one-foot diameter pipe filled with water, standing plumb or vertical, 545 feet tall. The bottom one foot of this pipe is going to see tremendous pressure, 245 psi to be exact. Remember, your car tire has 32 psi. It is this pressure, in tandem with the moving water, that will spin the turbine fins.

I have done some rough calculations. If I assume a flow rate of 200 gallons/ minute, figure in efficiency losses in the turbine and the generator, plus pipe friction, I should be able to produce 9,810 watts of power. My flow rate would allow me to operate for 285 days before depleting my reservoir. This assumes no additional rainfall. I could power 653 one-hundred-watt equivalent LED bulbs.

The cost to produce a project of this nature would likely exceed twenty-five million dollars. And how would I perch an

82,000,000-gallon basin on the side of a mountain? It would be an engineering marvel. The question that needs to be asked is, "Will this idea result in a meaningful ROI?" It is highly unlikely. We currently pay about $0.15 per KWH for electricity. If I were to do some quick math, it is likely my project would cost in excess of $150/ KWH. This project won't get off the ground, but wasn't it fun to try?

I know that this chapter is off the beaten path, and it was done intentionally. It could be beneficial to think outside the box. The science of physics can be our friend. We just need to try to understand it and channel its power to our advantage. And perhaps there are other resources one could farm. Maybe it doesn't need to be an apple or a carrot. How about harvesting stardust and moonbeams? Okay, I have gone too far!

FORTY-FOUR

Found It!

There are many ways to lose something and an infinite number of things to lose. I examine things that I have lost on the farm and then found or not.

There are many ways to lose something and an infinite number of things to lose. And there are many different incidents of loss. You could lose your way driving to your sister's new home, there is loss of a loved one, loss of a softball game, or lose your way in reading this book (I hope that is not happening!).

When I lost something on the farm, the search tactic would vary depending on what the object was and how large it was. In my early farm days, I plowed the fields a lot in preparation for new plantings. This was done by pulling a moldboard plow across the soil. The plow assembly could consist of one and up to about six moldboards per unit. Larger flat farms would often employ three- to six-bottom plows, but our small hilly farm was best served by using a two-bottom Dearborn 14" plow. The 14" dimension is the length of the plowshare. The share is the component of the plow, which meets the soil first and pulls the moldboards down into the earth, and the forward movement of the tractor/plow assembly causes the soil to flip over. The larger the share, the more soil can be turned over per pass. Rocks were plentiful on our hillside farm, and I marveled how there could be any left when looking at all the hundreds of thousands of stones forming walls around and through our farm.

The plow has two adjustments. One controls the bite by changing the front-to-back angle of the share, and the other affects the "roll" of the sod being turned over by the moldboard. The plow depth is controlled by the tractor driver. It is the engagement with rocks that causes the roll setting to change, and because there were many rocks still in the soil, my settings seemed to need frequent adjustments. These settings were adjusted by applying torque with a large wrench. The adjustment nuts were an inch and one-eighth across the hex. The adjustments became frequent enough that I needed to carry the 14" long wrench with me. Many tractors arrive from the factory without a toolbox, as was the case with our Massey Ferguson 50, so I simply rigged up a stiff wire with a "U" shape onto the plow and hung the closed end of the wrench onto it. This was a very handy arrangement until it wasn't. During one of the passes, the sod roll was off, which signaled it was time for an adjustment, but the wrench was gone. It must have been jarred off by one of the rock collisions, and now the wrench was lost. It was a $20 wrench, so it was worthy of a search. I walked back over the most recent pass but soon concluded that the search was in vain. The wrench was likely at the bottom of a furrow covered with ten inches of sod. It was lost!

Ten years later, I found the wrench. What were the odds of finding a piece of steel one inch wide and fourteen inches long lost in a three-acre field measuring 130,680 square feet?? It wasn't as though it was painted red, begging to be found. It would now be the same color as the soil from the rusting action over the years. I just happened to look down at the right place at the right time, and there it was!

Is there anyone who hasn't lost or misplaced their cell phone? You are likely to have left yours in a coat pocket or in the car console, and you find it. You employ a process of visualizing where and when you last remember using it and backtrack your steps until it is recovered. Losing a phone on a farm is different. While your recovery may have only taken fifty steps, our farm encompassed fifty-four acres. I lost and RECOVERED my little flip phone a dozen times. Some recoveries were quick, and some were not. I suspect those of us engaged in the occupation of farming incur a higher instance of phone losses than most others. In my case, being a tree fruit farmer, I was in regular physical contact with trees and their branches. Ascending and descending a ladder picking fruit or trimming a tree can, and has, ejected my phone from its sheath. Recovery, in this case, was relatively easy. I hadn't covered much real estate, and I could quickly retrace my steps and find it. The more challenging scenario was when a phone loss occurred while performing tractor activities.

Mowing our orchards took twelve hours. I lost my phone once or maybe twice while mowing. Usually, a mowing interval had occurred, the time one could comfortably sit on a tractor seat without needing a break before I noticed a phone missing incident. I checked for calls at noon or the end of the day, so four hours could pass before I realized the loss. Should there be a call, I couldn't hear the phone over the sound of the diesel engine and rarely felt the phone's vibration because the tractor's vibration cancels it. My recovery strategy in loss events via tractor was to get the four-wheeler out and drive up and down the mowed rows with MaryEllen's phone on speed dial to my number. I would stop at intervals, turn off the engine, and make the call, listening for my ringtone. For phone losses later in life, I have employed my hearing aids to improve recovery success.

The first farm product I could offer when we first purchased the farm was firewood. The western end of the farm contained a ten-acre woodlot. I visually surveyed the newly purchased forest and decided to start harvesting in its northwest corner. There was a group of twenty-inch diameter black oak trees ready for cutting. I could access the trees on foot with my chainsaw, but there was no way to get the cut wood out. There was a good logging road traversing the lot, north to south, on its east side of the woods, but there was no road to my wood quarry, so I would have to create one.

It looked as though the wood lot had not been logged in fifty years. I could find an occasional weathered and rotted stump, but clearly, there had been no cutting activity in decades. Besides the oak trees, there was also a sizable hemlock population, which I soon discovered had little value for logging purposes. I surveyed the lot's topography, seeking the best access route to the targeted oak trees. I needed to construct a road or path ten feet wide to accommodate a farm tractor towing a six-foot-wide trailer. The length of the new road would be about 300'. I fetched the chainsaw and started buzzing my way through toward my oak tree destination. This section of woods contained a combination of oak and hemlock trees varying in size from six to twelve inches in diameter. I made certain to cut the trees close to the ground so there would be no hang-ups traveling over the stumps with the tractor and trailer. In half a day's effort, the road was complete. As is the case with most farm tasks, I took the time to enjoy my accomplishment.

The point of the last two paragraphs was that I just found something. We could make an argument that it wasn't lost. As I peered down through my new road, I realized that I had found the original road to the northwest corner of the woodlot. The only reason I could make this claim is that now I could see the ruts in the soil created by earlier navigation through this section of woods. I found the original wood road!

I used to have 20/20 vision. Age happened, and a detached

Lost wood road

retina showed up, and now I need glasses, and I lose them from time to time. I suspect I have had more opportunity to lose my glasses than many of you who wear them. Mine got sprung from my face a minimum of six times per year. It was a big deal because they were expensive. I favored the Flexon brand because I could step on them, and they wouldn't break. Add in transitions for sun, progressive for reading, coating for durability, and, of course, the prescription, and I was presented with a bill for $900.

 I have developed a custom protocol that I employ when a loss event of this nature occurs. It's not a whole lot different than what a community might use to find a lost child. The searchers line up at a specific distance apart, all moving together in the same direction, covering a specific parcel of land. My loss incidents usually occurred while trimming an apple tree. A tree branch either plucked the glasses off or, in worse cases, the glasses were flung off by the energy in a compressed branch. Picture a sling shot here. In the scenario I am going to describe next, I was often perched on a ladder, twelve feet off the ground, clipping my way through the tree's canopy. So, a classic in-the-orchard loss goes like this: I am in an apple tree, removing excessive growth in preparation for the new growing season. Glasses are snagged from my face. I do an initial inspection around me, checking nearby branches and ladder rungs, hoping the glasses will be dangling within arm's reach. This never happens. Next, I descend the ladder and begin the ground search. The glasses will be directly below the ladder if it was a simple drop incident or somewhere within a ten-foot radius if I am dealing with a "fling" situation. The glasses won't be easy to find for two reasons. They will blend in well with leaves, twigs, and dirt, as the usual glass frame color is brushed steel. The second reason is I don't have my glasses! As in, I can't see. I methodically scan the ground around the ladder feet, being careful not to move my size thirteen feet until a scan is done. If there is no immediate recovery, I move to phase two. I scan the ground in increasingly larger concentric circles using the ladder as the focal point. This process always works, and I have always recovered my glasses.

In These Veins

Years ago, during the summer of 1972, it was necessary for me to make a business trip for IBM to its Boulder, Colorado plant. I was sent there to investigate quality issues with some computer components to be used in System 370 computers. This was my first professional field trip and my second year of employment at Big Blue's Poughkeepsie, NY plant, and I was going solo. I arrived and took care of business.

The Boulder plant sits on 464 acres of flat land at an elevation of 5,300'. On the second day of my visit, my IBM counterpart, Stan, offered to show me a bit of his state. We got permission to leave work a little early. I drove my rental car to a fringe area company parking lot to meet Stan. We departed on our excursion in his car. Our afternoon destination was Pikes Peak, about an hour and three-quarters away. We arrived at the Peak, got out of the car, marveled at the view, gasped for air (we were at an elevation of 14,115'), returned to the car, and headed back to the plant. We arrived at the parking lot at sunset. Stan dropped me off at my rental car, and he headed for home. A storm must have passed by while we were gone, as the parking lot was wet. As I approached my rental, I noticed the remains of a manila folder, now soggy, lodged against a tire. I unlocked the car to see my open briefcase on the passenger's seat. I quickly made the connection to the wet folder, and an awful feeling filled my belly.

The folder filled with IBM documents belonged in my briefcase. For some reason, I must have examined some documentation before Stan's arrival. I had likely become distracted by greeting him and inadvertently left the folder on top of my car. Neither Stan nor I noticed it before our excursion. Some of the folder contents were stamped "IBM Confidential," an intimidating designation to a newbie employee. The storm must have been accompanied by high winds as I couldn't find any document papers in my viewshed. There were no other cars in the lot. The papers were likely now lodged in a Kansas corn field. Kansas is due east of Colorado, and the prevailing wind is from the west. Darkness had now taken over the parking lot, the papers, and me. My first field trip, and I screwed up!

I got a grip on myself, drove over to the security hut, and reported my incident. I returned to work the next morning and met with Stan and his manager, Ralph. Security had contacted Ralph, and he had notified my manager back east. All the people who needed to know about the loss were informed.

Two months later, I was promoted to Associate Engineer. Part of the reason for my promotion had to do with my prompt reporting, honesty, and handling of the lost documents incident. I realize that I was unable to find the lost papers, but I would like to think those pages found their way to a farm in Kansas, and their recycled nutrients fed a few corn stalks.

Not all losses have to do with a thing or person, as in the loss of a loved one. Farmers can experience excessive swings in their net annual income during their agricultural career, usually induced by Mother Nature, unexpected insect issues, or falling commodity prices, often resulting in excessive stress, anxiety, or depression. I experienced a heavy dose of stress during the years from 1993 to 1996. At one point, I thought I may be LOSING my SANITY. My engineering position at IBM Poughkeepsie had been eliminated in the spring of 1993, resulting in my release from the company. Our farm was producing some income from our part-time efforts, but not enough to sustain us. I really did not want to pursue another engineering career, and this was an opportunity to farm full-time. We needed to expand production quickly to produce more income. We tapped into our meager savings to buy equipment, trees, vines, and a state-of-the-art irrigation system.

By 1995, the new crop production choices were yielding more than we had projected, which caught us off guard, and we lacked sufficient markets to sell our new products. I networked with a local vegetable farmer who graciously shared their customer list (we were selling fruit, so no conflict), all located ninety minutes south, dispersed throughout wealthy Westchester County. We made a reconnaissance trip to the customer list addresses, introduced ourselves and what we had to offer, and landed nine new customers! We hired more people, bought a delivery truck, and made improvements to our packing facility. I thought things were going along quite well, but I didn't feel "normal."

Thursday was our weekly delivery day to our Westchester markets, and on one Thursday morning in September of 1996, I found myself unable to complete my drive. I was traveling south on the New York State Thruway and had just passed through the Harriman toll booths. My mind became scrambled and disoriented, paired with a high dose of anxiety. I felt the need to exit the highway as quickly as possible to avoid causing an accident, which I was able to do at the conveniently placed Sloatsburg rest stop. I pulled over, parked, turned the truck off, and sat paralyzed for about a half hour. Was I losing my sanity? I had just experienced my first panic attack. I did some deep breathing and was able to restore some level of calmness and completed my delivery. Apparently, the changes I was experiencing on the farm had simply overwhelmed me. We had developed plans for expansion of our fruit production, invested considerable capital from our savings for equipment and infrastructure, and expended countless personal and employee hours implementing the buildout; but were we going to "make it" and be successful, or was I going to have to find a new job? These thoughts must have reached the boiling point in my mind on this particular day, and I reached my tipping point.

I soon made an appointment with my doctor, who prescribed one of those little pills to smooth the edges and calm me down. A few more attacks followed, but as time passed, I figured things out, got off the pills, and found my even keel again.

Earlier in this book, I wrote a chapter called Aardvark which is about a semi-ancient mechanical single-row corn picker. The inclusion of this paragraph and several to follow may seem out of place, but you will see why I have included them as you read on. I am very fond of this chapter, and I would like the reader to fully appreciate the design and appearance of this mechanical marvel. A photo of my machine would be helpful, but alas, I did not take one while it was passing through my ownership. So, you may want to suggest, "Doug, why not use the internet? There must be picker images somewhere in the cloud." Yes, in fact, there are many; however, my publisher was fearful of potential copyright issues. My best option would be to locate one of these agricultural antiques and snap a photo. I had been in contact with my friend Carmen, who owned Aardvark's sister in 1980, but his machine was long gone, and no photos were taken. I also checked in with another friend, Frank, thinking perhaps he would have seen one in his drives around the county, but no luck there. A Canadian traveling buddy, Ralph, who resides in Ontario, had seen one but, in his follow-up, was informed of the owner's passing, and apparently, the machine went with him to his grave. Farmers can become very attached to their machinery! I scoured Farm Bureau classifieds to no avail.

Opportunities to capture a legal photo of my beloved picker were not surfacing. I needed to expand the geographic reach of my search. It occurred to me that our Hudson Valley was simply too developed, and even though there are many thriving apple orchards, vineyards, and hemp plots, the propagation of corn for grain has dwindled. So, where should I target my search? Where do small farms still exist in greater numbers? I homed in on West Virginia, and bingo, I struck pay dirt in Union, West Virginia! I found an ag equipment dealer, David Atkins Farm Machinery, offering new and used farm machinery. I scrolled down through their listings and discovered no less than nine New Idea single-row corn pickers that looked just like my Aardvark. I emailed through their website and asked if it would be okay to stop by to snap a

Corn picker and me

photo or two of some pickers. Owner David Atkins responded, "Stop anytime, help yourself."

We quickly assembled plans to go to Union. And yes, I heard you sarcastically mumbling, "Why didn't you just call Mr. Atkins and ask him to take a couple of photos?" This thought did enter my mind; however, I had been looking for an excuse to shorten our winter and head somewhere warm like Savannah. Union was sort of on the way, and the hunt or quest, if you will, would be a mini adventure. We decided to drive, which has been our usual mode of transportation when heading south. We agreed to depart the next Thursday at 7 a.m. AIS (Ass In Seat, adopted from an episode of *Everybody Loves Raymond*). Thursday arrived, and we left at 7:09. MaryEllen was late. She had needed a few extra minutes to wipe down the kitchen island so she could return to a clean house. So much for our sacred AIS ritual!

After eight-and-a-half hours and 542 miles, we pulled into the Atkins yard. Our eyes quickly locked onto two of the sought-after pickers. We disembarked from our ride and strolled around the premise's perimeter, seeking other pickers to round out our photo choices, but found none. I was expecting to see nine options to depict the ideal New Idea image. The Atkins internet images needed updating to match their current inventory, but I am not complaining, and I am grateful there were two photo options. We snapped the needed photos, and now we're legal. Thank you, David!

I realize that this picker story does not fit the format of this chapter to a T, but the chance to land a photo had been exceptionally elusive, sort of lost, but I found it!

FORTY-FIVE

How Does a Farmer Retire?

The decision to retire from a career can be difficult for some people; it was for me, and then it wasn't. I detail events leading up to my decision to retire.

THE DECISION TO RETIRE FROM FARMING WAS DIfficult AT first. When I was in my late sixties, MaryEllen would regularly lean on me to make a plan for how and when to exit farming. I would spend some time pondering the idea but always came up empty.

I suspect most farmers are challenged with the concept of retiring. I believe it is easier to make this transition if there is a family member behind you. My daughter was clearly not interested and was following her own career path. My son showed interest for a while, but that faded over time and may have been influenced by me bitching too much about weather extremes, working too many hours, and low product prices.

The year 2018 rolled around, and we were still farming. I had always figured I would die on the farm, and my ashes would be used to fertilize a peach tree. It seemed MaryEllen's plan to get me to retire was a fairytale. That was about to change. We started with normal weather in 2018. If you are a farmer reading this, you know that "normal weather" is an oxymoron. I have held the belief that a normal year in agriculture is an imaginary condition and is arrived at by averaging the extremes that occur. In late summer, rainy days were on the increase. Normal rainfall in our part of New York is about forty inches, but this year, it was going to be more like sixty. Most of the excess fell in September and October when apples and grapes were harvested.

It rained every other day, with the period featuring cool temperatures and overcast skies. I am a sunny-day person, so my daily mood was not cheerful, and I could feel a little depression nagging at me.

Most of the fruit was moved from the field to the farmyard via wooden twenty-bushel bins for apples or one-ton plastic bins for the wine grapes. Many years ago, I had designed and fabricated a set of adjustable forks that could be mounted on the rear of a tractor using its three-point lift system. I could adjust the attitude or angle, always keeping the bin of fruit level. There were two issues with this approach. My neck and spine got a workout being twisted to the rear, observing how the bin was behaving during transport. The other issue was that there was too much sway, causing the bin to lurch from side to side. There was more than one situation where the "lurch" caused the bin to fall off the forks, leaving 800 pounds of fruit on the ground. I found over time that it was more efficient to transport the bins with front forks on our New Holland TN70. It provided a more stable trip down our mountain farm, and I could see what the bin was doing and adjust its inclination as needed. I never lost a bin off of the front forks.

Navigating on our farm roads was never an issue, but in wet tree and vineyard rows, the rules are different. Most of our rows were planted in a north-to-south orientation, perpendicular to the east-to-west mountain descending hillside. These north-south row plantings provided the best light reception for the fruit and the safest navigation with equipment.

The constant rain soon put the soil into a saturated condition, causing instability to its structure and yielding unpredictable navigation across it. Any attempt to make a second pass in the same row only led to producing muddy ruts. These were the conditions that separated the men from the boys, experienced versus newbie, veteran versus rookie. This was a year where you could not travel in the same row twice without creating eternal ruts.

The front tires of the TN were nearly bald, hence very low traction. I found myself continuously riding a left or right brake just to stay on the mountain. (Yes, tractors have left and right brakes.)

To compound this sour season, our local cider mill threatened to stop taking apple culls because of low sugar content. Cool, wet, sunless days cause a reduction in fruit sugar. Normally, an apple achieves a Brix level approaching 15, but this year, they were testing at 10. My emotional stress level was on the rise. Taking the edge off this lousy season could be easy; after all, we did own a winery. The TTB wouldn't mind. By upwardly adjusting that line called "family use" in the annual TTB report, we could easily imbibe a little more, and Uncle Sam would be okay with it.

By the end of that harvest season, I was not in a happy place, and my spirit had been compromised. I was seventy years old at this point, and we were financially secure. The playing field seemed to have changed in a few months. A short while ago, I was going to farm forever and become fertilizer for a peach tree, but suddenly, I seemed ready to consider an exit from farming. One day, I said to MaryEllen, "Something has to change. This winter, we need to talk about this thing called retirement."

We finished out the year. When the new year came around, and with this new concept of retirement fresh on my mind, we decided to hire a consultant to help us with our future in farming.

I asked him to frame out three different scenarios. Should we have someone manage the business, take on a partner, or sell. He asked us lots of questions. He went off to do his analysis and returned a couple of weeks later. He described the pros and cons of the three options but felt that the sell option would be the best. The ball was now in our court.

In recent years, we have been taking a winter vacation. We tend to seek out warmer climates, and Savannah had risen to be our go-to destination, so we made plans to go in February 2019. This trip started off a little differently. We had some analysis to do. During our life together, MaryEllen and I have often made important decisions by making a spreadsheet listing all possible options and then the pros and cons of each. This was going to be a life-changing decision, and we needed to give it our due diligence.

It's a two-day car drive from Marlboro to Savannah. Only in motion for an hour, MaryEllen turned to me and said, "We know what we have to do. Are you ready?" I said, "Let's get started." Our page headings were "Hire Manager," "Take on Partner," and "Sell." After twenty hours in the car over the course of two days, I think we had filled up nine pages of pros and cons. When we reached our destination, had settled into our room, and poured a glass of wine, MaryEllen said, "I can't think of anything else to add. Can you?" I shook my head. And then she asked me, "What do you think we should do?" Without any hesitation, I said, "It's obvious. We're going to sell." A heavy burden seemed to lighten almost immediately. It was that simple. A life-changing decision was made in two days.

We returned home a week later, ready to make things happen and move quickly. With the decision to retire and sell the farm fresh in our minds, we needed a realtor to help make it happen. We interviewed three real estate agencies and selected one. Our farm sale was posted, and within two months, we had an offer. The sale was consummated in January of 2020. Holy crap, we did it!

FORTY-SIX

Paradise

*I never thought I would be building
a new home at the age of seventy-two, but it is,
in fact, what we did. There clearly is life after
retirement, and we are living in Paradise!*

RETIREMENT WAS ON OUR DOORSTEP, AND WE HAD TO MOVE. I had lived on our land for forty-one years, MaryEllen for twenty-seven, and now we had to decide where to go. More on that in a moment. The immediate issue was what I was going to do with my newfound time. How was I going to migrate from working seventy hours a week to having every day free? During the last twenty years, I have entertained the concept of pursuing other business ventures. I would have liked to own a hardware store, a wine shop, or an art gallery, be a wine importer or a house renovator. I would now have the time to follow up with one of these ideas. But in reality, at my age, these were not practical paths to go down, and I did not want to become a two-time divorcé! These endeavors would have to remain as fantasies or perhaps for another lifetime.

I was about to enter this newly created space, which featured a significant reduction of responsibility, and that felt good. I heard myself saying in my mind and even vocalized to MaryEllen that I would like to practice being irresponsible. This may have been a noble goal, but it was not plausible because my responsibility gene would be difficult to suppress.

I expected to live for another twenty to twenty-five more years, or to say it another way, a quarter of my life could still be ahead of me, so I had better fill it with meaningful events or endeavors. My health had been good to this point, and there were no known issues. I knew I wanted to remain healthy in body, mind, and spirit. I adopted a couple of cardiovascular routines nudged on by my newly assigned cardiologist. During the retirement decision process, I developed an arrhythmia condition, so I was asked to undergo a few diagnostic tests. The erratic heart condition resolved itself once I was comfortable with my retirement decision.

This newfound workless space would also permit me to think, develop better-informed opinions, and educate myself on just about anything. I knew I wanted to be exposed to new experiences that didn't need to include bungee jumping or a trip to the edge of space. I could now participate in a political caucus, witness live thoroughbreds galloping at Saratoga race track, or go to the New York State Fair. The possibilities were endless, and it felt great!

MaryEllen and I discussed the usual things retired couples do, like traveling to new places in the States, visiting foreign countries, riding our bikes around the local counties, eating out more, and visiting friends and family more frequently.

We spent a lot of time talking about where we might move to. France and Italy were options. Their reputation for great wine is no secret, but Europe would be too large a leap. And, of course, awesome wines are crafted right here in New York. We realized we had the opportunity to move out of New York, commonly known as "the land of high taxes." Two times a year, the tax bills show up, one for the school district and then the municipal bill. The municipal bill was reasonable, but the school bill was pretty scary, high enough for us to consider finding a more tax-friendly state.

We found Zillow very helpful in researching other states from the comfort of home. Everywhere is less expensive than our Hudson Valley. We considered Georgia, South Carolina, Virginia, Tennessee, and Pennsylvania. All these areas have a more favorable cost of living. On the other hand, both MaryEllen and I were born and raised here in the Hudson Valley; we live three miles from the Hudson River. The Valley has a wonderful diversity of people, natural beauty, family, and distinct seasons, and it's impossible to beat the autumn colors. Our lifelong accumulation of friends also live here.

We weighed our options and eventually decided to stay in New York. We scoured nearby Orange County and our own Ulster County for ranch homes and single-story living. A month of searching only revealed a handful of choices, and nothing really attracted us except for one home. We looked at it and liked it very much. It was twenty-five years old, in great shape, and just about five miles down the road from the farm. The house had pretty much everything we were looking for, including a full basement. It sat on three acres with mature landscaping, and it included an empty parcel directly across the street, which guaranteed a vast view shed; from the house, we could see the Hudson River and Bannerman's Island. We thought we might have found our house. We visited it with the realtor twice and liked it enough to liquidate a couple of accounts so we'd have a down payment ready, but we couldn't quite seem to pull the trigger. We struggled to figure out what was holding us back. We tried imagining ourselves there, and we thought we'd be very comfortable until one day, I thought to myself, *Suppose I wanted to plant a tree, and when I dug the hole, I pulled out a couple of large rocks. Where would I put those rocks?* And that's when the light bulb came on. There wouldn't be any place to put those rocks because the three acres were all manicured.

It was just a little too polished and perfect for us. And honestly, I knew I would need more than three acres to keep me busy in retirement, even without actively farming. We were now realizing it was quite likely we would have to build our own home.

Our land search was compounded because we also realized we desired a view very much like the one we already had. Our old farm bordered another farm directly south. It's a thirty-six-acre parcel on top of the mountain with an awesome view. The property sits at an elevation of 850' above sea level, which gives it an advantage. We could imagine two potential house sites. Both sites were at the north end of the property and nearly at the highest point on the farm. One could be backed up against some woods, and the other could be more centrally positioned. Either one would give us a 1,000-foot internal farm view. Both would give us a thirty-mile view to the east, peering out at the Taconic Mountain range. We had considered buying this parcel during the past twenty years but always let the thought fade. We didn't need more land to farm. I had floated the idea of purchasing the farm a few years back, but MaryEllen wisely pointed out that I had all I could do to handle what we had, and she put the kibosh on the idea.

But once we decided to sell our farm, this new farm was viewed in a new light. We didn't have to farm it, just enjoy it. One day, I asked MaryEllen to go for a ride with me without telling her where I was taking her. Once I made the turn up the mountain, she knew exactly where we were going. I wanted her to see what I saw in this farm. It must have worked. I convinced MaryEllen that we should try to buy it. We made an offer, and it was accepted. We closed on the property on August 21, 2019.

Although the new farm had no formal home on it, it did have a migrant labor camp house, but it was small, too close to the town road, and would need considerable renovation, so that option quickly fell out of consideration.

We knew we wanted a home all on one level, an age-in-place

home, if you will, ideally with no more than two steps to enter. Some would describe it as a "toes up" house. So here we were making plans to build a new home; a few short months ago, it wasn't even on our radar. Less than a year later, we were in our beautiful new home with a view from every room. We call our new home and farm Paradise.

FORTY-SEVEN

D3

For some people—not just farmers—operating large pieces of equipment is exhilarating. I enlighten the reader to the experience of driving a D3 Caterpillar.

There is a saying, "You can take the boy off the farm, but you can't take the farm out of the boy." Farming is in my veins. I am seventy-six, and I can't wait until tomorrow to sit on a tractor, dig in the dirt, and plant something. When we sold our fruit farm, I took three tractors with me, bought another, and also picked up a Bobcat E35 excavator. One can't have too many tractors. The one void I felt was that I did not have a bulldozer. I believe the Caterpillar brand is the best, and for our farm, the model D3 would be perfect. I searched for one for a year and a half with no luck. Every farmer with dirt under his fingernails and probably some in his veins wants to own a dozer, though the favored brand and size will vary.

We were fortunate to have found a respected builder for our house. He has since become a great friend. Andy has a D3, and although he won't sell it, he let me borrow it! We did the deal by way of a barter. Andy gets to hunt whitetail deer on our farm, and I get to use his D3. The barter system is a great way to secure goods and services without writing a check.

There were 600 old apple trees on our new farm. Most of them were twenty feet tall and ugly as they had not been tended to in four years. Apple trees left to go wild have no visual appeal. Disease and insects take over, and by August, the leaves are dropping. These antique trees just didn't add to the beauty of our viewshed.

We consummated the barter arrangement, and Andy arranged the delivery of the dozer—all 17,000 pounds. This machine likely came off the assembly line in the 1990s. The beauty of this little beast is its simplicity. All the gauges are analog, signaling oil pressure, water temperature, and amperage. There is no clutch and no steering wheel; navigation is done by left and right foot brakes. There are two gear ranges with three speeds each plus reverse. Top speed is 7.1 mph. There is no chance of a digital technology failure because there is no digital technology on it. Blade positions are changed by one simple joystick. By the way, dozers are measured by how much they weigh; the heavier they are, the more they can push. I had only been on a dozer once before. It was about fifty-five years ago at my uncle's farm. It was a small Allis Chalmers. I used it for about an hour until one of the tracks fell off. The image of that experience stayed with me, and I hoped not to repeat it with Andy's dozer.

I could sense the fear in the orchard; I thought I could make out some frowning faces on some of the tree trunks. The D3 was parked at the edge of the oldest block. The trees seemed to lean in as if to get a better look at the mustard-colored mountain of steel attached to the ground with caterpillar-like iron feet, or maybe it was the stiff west wind fooling my eyes.

The dozer sat idle for a couple of days. We had gotten a good dose of rain recently, and the soil needed to dry a bit. I used the time to assess which block to push first and where to construct the resulting piles of wood.

D3 and me

A few days later, I was ready to go. The image you need to place in your mind is this: Picture a three-year-old child peering into the living room on Christmas morning to see his or her bright green John Deere tricycle tractor. That's exactly how I felt as I inserted the key into the Cat.

I donned my sound muffs and let the machine warm up. I brought the throttle up to a roar, probably to 2,500 to 3,000 rpm. To my surprise, it had no tachometer. I made my way into the tree block, steering with braking foot pedals. The D3 was roaring, moving at the lightning speed of one-half mile per hour, with its sight drawing a bead on the first tree. The blade made contact with the trunk, and with very little effort, the tree slowly tipped over, the roots giving way from their sixty-year grip on the soil.

The process seemed daunting at first as I didn't have a clue as to how long it would take to topple all these trees. As each hour passed, my efficiency improved. I was soon popping out a tree every minute. In less than twenty hours, there were 500 trees lying on their sides. We decided to leave about a hundred trees to maintain some visual texture in our viewshed.

The more difficult task remained. What does one do with the 500 downed trees? I could find a corner of the farm and push the trees to a compressed pile, then wait five years until the dead cellulose melts into the earth. This is commonly done when a farmer has sufficient space, and this is, in fact, what I did with some of the trees. The D3 was up for a seven-tree push per pass. Adding the eighth tree would cause tracks to spin and no forward motion. A new skill set was needed for the push process. It was essential to find the right push point to balance root mass and branch volume. I soon mastered the push routine, and the fields cleaned up quickly.

There was a limit as to how far to push the trees. Other portions of the farm were in excess of 500 feet from our new tree graveyard. I decided that it would be more practical to pile the trees in their respective blocks, let them dry, and then burn them at a later date.

I was able to clear and pile our aging orchard in forty hours. It was a lot less time than I expected! It was at this point a sadness began creeping over me. My dozer work seemed to be complete. Will I now still be able to justify my own D3? Only time will tell, but it does not look very promising.

FORTY-EIGHT

Seeking Success

*"Some people dream of success while
others wake up and work hard at it."*

"Some people dream of success while others wake up and work hard at it." This is not my saying—it was Napoleon Hill's—but I refer to it on occasion. I am not very fond of failure and put in considerable effort to avoid it. To be blunt, I'm not built for failure; it's not in my DNA. We have been fortunate to experience many successes during our farming career. Our planning efforts and hard work paid off. Striving for success is the best attitude to have, but I suppose one should be prepared for an occasional upset. They should rarely occur if the planning and execution are done well. This is not to say that I haven't experienced failure. There have been some minor events and one major.

Our investment in a cider company was a biggie. We thought it would be a good idea to be financially diversified. The current partners were mostly known to us, and we could sell some of our apples to the mill. As time passed, we realized that we had not done enough research about how this market worked and how to expand it, and we didn't foresee how powerful our competition was. Eventually, we were squeezed out of business through deliberate low pricing. We tried to match prices, but margins were too thin, and the company failed. All our investment money was lost. Ouch!

When I was laid off by IBM in 1993, we tried planting several new fruits. There wasn't a lot of time to perform in-depth research. We were attempting to ramp up fresh income quickly. I had gone from a weekly paycheck to none. Don't get too teary-eyed, as I received a decent buyout package that helped tide us over. Strawberries are a fruit that can produce a commercial crop in their second year. Technically, in one year, we should be rolling in money. The "quick" plan did not go so well. I did a poor job preparing the soil ahead of the planting. The plot should have been limed, plowed, disked, and spring-toothed. Instead, I chose to take a shortcut and just run a cultivator across it a couple of times. Weeds were a major problem during year two, and once established, they were difficult to suppress as the strawberry plants started to advance. If I had plowed and prepped the field before planting, the weeds would have been buried. My shortcut cultivating approach seemed to transplant the weeds.

But the weeds did not do us in. It was a plant disease. I was not prepared with the plant-specific knowledge, nor did I possess the proper equipment. And the fact that the berries get picked just two inches off the ground did not help. Humans are not designed to be bent at right angles for more than a couple of minutes. After a dismal harvest in the second year, we decided to bag it. This was a failure!

I have been farming professionally for over forty years and have acquired considerable experience and knowledge during my journey. And yet, I am right now perched on the precipice of a potential failure.

I decided to plant Christmas trees on our retirement farm in 2020. I had planted a couple thousand during the early years at our old farm. I am not new at this; it should be like riding a bike.

My targeted tree plot is in the center of the farm, a field that we have since named Blue Flats. The location of the planting was determined mostly by aesthetic values. We wanted to be able to gaze out from our house and view a sea of year-round greenery. The site is nearly flat with only a one- to two-degree slope. I researched our farm soil types, which told us that Blue Flats is made up of Volusia soil. It is my understanding that ninety percent of U.S. soils have been classified. To make soil research even easier, I found an app for my phone (I changed out my flip phone) whereby I can stand on any soil surface and be told what soil type is beneath me. I had never come across Volusia soil during my farming journey. The top eight inches are black and fluffy and very fertile looking. There is also a good dose of stones and shale shards mixed in. The next twenty inches consist of clay soil, which implies high water retention properties. The trees to be planted here are blue spruce, as they are deer-resistant. I checked to see what type of soil blue spruce are happy in, and it turns out they're okay with moist but not wet soil. Clay is not their first choice, but they will grow in it, albeit more slowly. They prefer a pH of 5.5 to 7.0.

A test of the soil's pH came back at 5.5. Since that's the lower end of the spruces' happy zone, I applied lime to sweeten the soil. I did not re-test, but the pH should have improved to about 5.7.

I noticed that water would linger on the soil surface after a meaningful rain. Essentially, the soil stayed wet for a week. This was not good as these trees don't like wet feet, so I decided to install drainage. I was trying to give these trees every opportunity to flourish. I got my transit out to ensure there was a continuous slope moving away from the site. I installed three lines spaced twenty feet apart with a perforated pipe in the bottom and added stone from bottom to top. Standing water had nowhere to go but down. I disked the surface smooth, and we were ready to plant.

In April 2020, 175 blue spruces arrived. I laid out the plot with rows eight feet apart. I ripped a thin line in the soil about one foot deep. The tree size varied considerably. Some were so small that if I laid one on the ground, looked away, and then back, I couldn't find it. Others were fourteen inches tall with many roots. The trees were in their dormant state with buds still closed.

I stuffed the tree roots into the soil slits at eight-foot intervals, then closed the slits, pushing earth against the roots, driving out any air from contact with the roots. This is a critical step in the planting process.

I now waited to see what the "take" would be, meaning how many trees take off and live and how many don't. There were some dry periods during which I added water. By July, the results were in. If there is a ninety percent take rate, I call it a success. I made the count, which yielded a sixty-seven percent mortality rate, or a measly thirty-three percent take rate. What had gone wrong? I suspected the high mortality had to do with poor row closure around the large-rooted trees, and the initial row ripping was likely too deep. The "ripping" process is achieved by pulling a tractor-mounted subsoiler through the soil resulting in a slit in the earth. The slit can be shallow or deep depending on where one sets the height control. I suspect my rip was too deep, making it difficult to apply enough down-hand pressure to squeeze out all of the air in the tree root zone. We probably should pause here and define "failure." Failure is the inability to meet expectations. It sure looked like a failure, but I was not ready to give up for one reason: I hadn't specified a timeline.

In the fall, I re-ordered 200 trees but made two changes. All the trees would be smaller and single-rooted for ease of planting, and I scheduled the delivery for May 20. This is much later than normal. I had chosen the late date because the extra trees, the spares, were to be planted in the garden. The garden would do double duty. It would grow our summer veggies and serve as a nursery. I was going to mature the baby trees for transplant to other parts of the farm next year. Due to frosts and low soil temperatures, the garden gets prepped and planted in late May. I attempted to match the tree arrival with the garden prep. Big mistake! The trees arrived as requested. I opened the box to find the little tikes already growing. The trees had broken dormancy, with buds burst open and new green tissue beginning to grow. Not good! You might think that the nursery should take some responsibility, but not in this case, as I chose the late ship date.

I had no choice but to plant the trees. I re-populated all the dead positions in Blue Flats and made sure all the air was pushed out from around the roots. I even added drip irrigation in every row. I did not have to wait long to declare their fate. Nearly every tree died. The tender new growth succumbed to the late spring sun, which essentially fried them. I now had two sequential blunder-filled years under my belt. It felt like I was witnessing a failure in slow motion. Was I headed for failure? But not so fast; I wasn't giving up.

I am not certain that I will be able to report the fate of Blue Flats before this book goes to press. The success/failure declaration has yet to be determined. The trees have been reordered for the second time. The delivery date is for the first week in April. I'm rooting for success.

FORTY-NINE

Save The Ridge

Many municipalities enact laws to protect the environment and natural beauty assets. Our town debates the need for them.

MaryEllen and I recently returned from a Viking cruise, which began in Greece and finished in Venice. We had been asked by traveling buddies, a married couple, if we would like to join them and some of their family members to celebrate the couple's fiftieth wedding anniversary. The cruise began in Athens, and on one of our guided bus sightseeing days, on our way to see one of the many archeological sites, our tour guide called our attention to the fact that no building in Athens may exceed twelve stories in height. This building code was initiated so that the view of the 2,460-year-old Acropolis, a UNESCO World Heritage Site, would remain unimpeded. The code was put in place for the greater good of the city and its many visitors, though perhaps to the detriment of local developers' potential profits.

As I type these sentences, I see a lively debate occurring on social media and at official town meetings concerning the removal of a local law. The Town of Marlborough adopted its first Comprehensive Master Plan in 2002. One of the aspects of the plan identified The Marlboro Mountain Ridgeline as a natural treasure and stated that measures should be taken to protect it. In 2005, Local Law 155-41.1 was enacted to provide protection for the Ridgeline view and its soils. The law affects land parcels of 750' elevation and higher located in the Ridgeline Overlay Protection Area. A map was created to depict this geographic area. The Marlboro Mountains were created 10,000 years ago during the Ice Age and traverse from south to north for 7.7 miles, beginning at the Orange County border and ending at the Town of Lloyd. I have hiked the ridgeline many times, and I find it to be a magical monument to quiet. It is void of voices and the drone of auto tires. One only sees trees, rock, drifted spent leaves, and mossy earth, much the way it has been for hundreds of centuries. The eighty-foot oak tree canopies are home to owls, hawks, and bald eagles. I wonder what would happen to these magnificent creatures if houses were permitted on the ridgeline.

The Marlboro Mountains are the watershed for a robust 5,700-acre agricultural area. The highest peaks on the ridge reach a few feet over 1,000 feet in elevation. The views of the ridge from the east and from the ridge to the east are stunning. The majestic Hudson River, first named the North River, is just three miles to the east, and if you were standing on the ridge in 1609, you could have seen Henry Hudson's ship, the Half Moon, sailing north toward what is now James Bay, Canada. Settlers arrived in our community around 1697, so the ridge has remained essentially houseless for over 325 years.

Marlboro has been blessed with many productive farms that grow state-of-the-art apple tree plantings, wine grape vineyards, plus acres of various vegetables. Farms, by their very nature, provide open space for everyone to view and enjoy; however, there is always pressure from individuals and companies to develop these open spaces, and they have the right to pursue opportunities that may arise.

During the latter part of 2023, a landowner in the Ridgeline Overlay Protection Area was proceeding with plans to erect a home on the ridge. The ridgeline law of 2005 states that one is not permitted to erect a structure within fifty vertical feet of the ridgeline in the overlay area. The appropriate municipal authorities were consulted, and upon evaluation, the applicant was denied approval. Essentially, the law permits a structure to be placed on the side of the mountain but not on top of the mountain. The law has some ambiguity in its language as it uses the terms "treeline" and "ridgeline" in the same paragraph, which is easily corrected while still retaining the elevation setback.

For reasons not clear to me, the town board decided to change the law and eliminate the fifty-foot buffer. They offered a period of time to accept public comments, which precipitated a lively townwide debate both on social media and live at public forums. Sides and positions were quickly taken, one for keeping the ridge view natural without homes on it and the other promoting land rights, which basically comes down to one being able to do whatever one wishes with one's property. MaryEllen and I have taken the position that the fifty-foot buffer should remain in place, protecting the ridge view, which would be for the greater good of the community and its visitors. If the view of the 2,460-year-old Acropolis is worth saving, why wouldn't the view of our 10,000-year-old mountain? As of this writing, no decision has been made.

FIFTY

Savor Simple

Most rewards gleaned from a farm are not related to money.

THIS BOOK STARTED OUT AS A MEMOIR BUT BECAME MORE AS I transferred my memories from my brain to text. It is, in fact, the story of my agricultural life, but as I developed my stories, I found myself needing to educate the reader about how and why things are done on a small American farm. It could, in some ways, be considered a template for farm living. Some may see it as an Americana documentary. We humans are uniquely different from other forms of life because we are able to write down our thoughts and memories. I believe it is important for us to document from time to time to preserve the history of our culture. I have attempted to achieve that concept throughout the previous chapters.

Life was much simpler seventy years ago, but it is relative because seventy years from now, people may say to each other, "What was that thing called AI, artificial intelligence?" Farm life and the experiences in it don't need to be complicated. If we step away from technology, social media, politics, and the price of commodities, there are thousands of moments a farmer can revel in along his or her agriculture journey. Have you ever watched a honey bee hover and land on a flower? I have pruned thousands of peach trees, which is done during their May bloom cycle, and I shared the trees' space with bees as they floated from blossom to blossom, gathering pollen and nectar. On a perfect seventy-degree windless day, there can be a hundred of these fuzzy gold, black-striped creatures hovering amidst the trees' air space, seeking their meal for the day. If you were to pause for a moment, you would notice that the tree took on a "hum" of its own. I believe if I could record and amplify their harmonic buzz, it could be music for meditation.

Do you know what a tendril is? It is a twisting, clinging, slender, coil-like structure on grapevines. It starts off green in color, changes to brown at the end of the season, and is similar in size to pencil lead. Tendrils attach themselves to a trellis or post to provide support for the plant and, once lignified, are nearly impossible to remove without severing with hand shears. I have studied these supple, green, natural wires too many times to count. I believe it takes less than a day for a tendril to make a single revolution around a grape trellis wire. Next time you are in a vineyard in July, try taking a time-elapsed video and see if you can prove me wrong. I know this is silly, stupid shit, but I love it!

I believe that one of the simplest forms of gratification on a farm is to accomplish a task. You define a task, make a plan, execute the plan, and reap the reward every day! It might be mowing a hay field, trimming a row of grapes, shearing a hundred sheep, or planting a new acre of orchard. The feeling of accomplishment is stimulating and never gets old for me.

In the chapter "The Massey Ferguson," I spoke about plowing a field and reveling in the fact that I could see exactly where I had been and enjoy my progress across the field with each plow passage. I neglected to share with you two additional observations

I made that day. The plowing process, or the flipping or rolling over of sod and soil, produces a unique, natural perfume called geosmin. It is literally the smell of fresh earth with a hint of mushroom and schist, enhanced by friendly microbes and bacteria. It's just one of those intangible rewards one experiences when racing around a field at one mile per hour. It is not likely, though, to become the next Chanel scent blockbuster. And, oh yes, the second observation of that plow day was that a red fox followed me up and down the freshly made furrows seeking newly released field mice. These are the simple rewards you won't find anywhere but on a farm.

There is a small pond near the center of our retirement farm. It measured about 100' by 100' when we first took possession of the land—small by most standards. It was once the irrigation source for the farm. While the excavator machine was on the premises for site work for our new home, I asked the operator to enlarge the pond, which now feels as though it was a mistake. I will explain shortly. The pond is flanked by tall poplar trees on its northeast corner and on the south. Reeds border the northwest corner; the remainder abuts shoreline grasses.

The first summer after we moved into our new home, we adopted a routine of visiting the pond on Fridays at 5 PM during the warm months. I painted the simple description of the pond setting because that is exactly what it is—simple. We visit there with a cold bottle of white wine and linger for about an hour perched on two seven-dollar Home Depot plastic chairs, one white and the other pink; no cell phones are permitted. We sit quietly on the pond bank, with a pair of binoculars handy, to observe and listen to whatever the space offers us.

On one of our first Friday visits, we were greeted by a large snapping turtle, still wet, probably a female, headed for higher ground to lay her eggs. During the first year of our routine, we witnessed two to three turtle heads intermittently poke through the water's surface. We haven't seen any snappers since. I suspect the excavator removed too much of the pond's mud, which also doubled as the turtle's security blanket. We only see painted turtles these days and miss our beloved snappers.

Over the course of the viewing season, we see and hear mockingbirds, red-winged blackbirds, goldfinches, and a host of others. Once, a hen turkey and her flock of poults strutted by. Another time, a doe deer stopped mid-gallop to inspect her intruders. In early August, blue-winged darning needles hover and dart all about us. Largemouth bass leap from the pond, hoping to score a floating insect. Numerous rainbows have lifted our spirits over the years. Hidden frogs croak from reeds and grasses. By this time, you're likely nearly asleep, and I am not going to apologize. We savor this simple hour together, and perhaps you will consider it as well.

Epilogue

WHY DO I FARM? IN SHORT, I CAN'T HELP MYSELF; IT'S IN MY veins, my DNA, and in the fiber of my soul. I have always been lured to the earth and revel in what can be grown in it and on it. I believe it comes down to simply being able to create something, nurturing it, and watching it grow. It could be and has been things like waiting for my first turtle egg to hatch on my mini turtle farm when I was seven, watching the baby chicks grow into egg layers, or raising a two-day-old calf into a 1,600-pound steer. I have watched four-inch seedling blue spruce trees grow to be forty feet tall, a three-foot-high apple tree grow to produce fifteen bushels of apples, and the tomato plant spindle produce that daily summer tomato sandwich. It really doesn't matter what the medium is; if I can grow it, I'm a happy person. I have often said I don't need cocaine to get high; farming is my drug.

There are other peripheral aspects of farming that are rewarding as well. We grew peaches on our farm along with our pears, apples, and wine grapes. People seem to love peaches. We would grow them such that when you chomped down on one, you needed a napkin to protect yourself from the abundant, sweet, fragrant juice. They were bursting with flavor and aroma. People would say, "Doug, you will have these next week, right? My sister is visiting from Syracuse next Tuesday, and she will want to stock up." We always prided ourselves in picking our fruit at its peak flavor. Even going into the cooler to fetch a load for the market was rewarding as the room oozed the aroma of peaches.

Along the way, I learned many new skills, which is satisfying in itself. I know how to repair a New Idea corn picker. I can weld my moldboard plow back together. Grafting a new shoot onto an apple stump is no longer a mystery. I can fell a twenty-inch oak tree right where I want it; well, okay, not always. If you ever need assistance with your calf birthing, just give me a shout. I could tell you how to not break a rib, but you will break one anyway. Building stone walls and constructing French drains could now be my next career. If you need masonry stonework for your fireplace surround or chimney, I'm your man. I have become quite adept at interpreting a weather forecast. There is even a knack for starting a fire in a brush pile, and I've mastered that. Need help to pick out your next wife?

I think farmers are special people. They talk slower, they are patient, and they listen to reason, logic, and science. Farmers are great planners as they need to project what they should be growing five to ten years down the road. They don't physically move very fast but tend to get where they need to be. I enjoy being around them, and I'm happy to be one.

Innovation is no stranger to the farmer either. We are savvy in applying the latest research from agricultural universities. I was always eager to try a new approach if it was appropriate for our farm. Very early on, we adopted the concept of water conservation and installed a drip irrigation system that uses a fraction of the water that an overhead system uses. It felt good to have done this as it not only helped us grow larger fruit but is beneficial to the planet as well. We migrated to more efficient planting systems, which enabled us to become profitable more quickly. Changes like these were not only good for the bottom line but were mentally stimulating to learn something new and witness the positive results.

There is also a larger role that farmers play that they quite likely do not spend much time pondering about. The mere fact that they own the area the farm sits on should be considered preserving open space. People generally adore this concept. People would much rather have a farm in their viewshed than other houses or backyards. Towns, counties, and states will even pay farmers to keep their land free of development in the form of easements or sale of development rights. We tried to do this but failed because towns tend to want to preserve large parcels and parcels that can be hooked together; ours was not large enough or near other land preservation candidates.

And then, there is this concept of climate change. Not everyone will agree, but data seems to indicate that our planet is getting hotter. Trapped carbon dioxide gasses in our atmosphere contribute to rising global temperatures. Farmers, not knowingly, are maintaining some stability in the ecosystem. Farm-grown trees, vines, plants, grains, and grasses all perform a form of carbon dioxide cleaning. They also produce oxygen, which is needed by all forms of life, as part of their photosynthesis process. Farmers don't leave their houses each morning saying, "My goal today is to capture twenty-five tons of CO_2." It is simply an unintended byproduct of what they do.

I love to farm and intend to continue to be a part of the noble profession of farming for as long as I am able. As long as I can walk and climb into my tractor, I will be a farmer.

Ten Reasons to Become a Farmer

(DOUG GLORIE—FEBRUARY 2010)

1. You will witness many sunrises.
2. You will become an active environmentalist.
3. You will produce safe food products made in the USA.
4. You will feel the earth give beneath your feet.
5. You will provide local employment and not be exporting an American job.
6. You will create thousands of pieces of artwork annually when trimming trees and vines.
7. You will eliminate, or at least postpone, a housing development.
8. Your land taxes will go down.
9. You will acquire skills that you did not know existed.
10. You will develop a new sensitivity for Mother Nature.

Farm Glossary

*Farm and Winery Words
and Terms Used on Our Farm*

Accipiter: Name for the genus of birds of prey—hawks—often seen on our farm.

Acetobacter: A bacteria that can be present in wine and cause it to spoil.

Amelioration: The process of adding water to wine before fermentation to reduce acidity. This was never done at Glorie Farm Winery.

Angel's Share: The evaporation of wine or spirits from an oak barrel.

Anther: The pollen producing part of a flower.

Ascospore: First stage in the growth of apple scab disease, which occurs every spring in most northeastern orchards.

Baccalà: Salted cod prepared in our kitchen annually at the completion of my Italian friends' slaughter of their beef cow. It is a food that wife number two warned me should not enter her kitchen.

Brown Snout: An antique apple variety.

Cambium: The layer of plant tissue responsible for the secondary growth of roots and stems.

Carpe Diem: From Latin meaning "Seize the day." An expression we adopted in the early nineties to remind ourselves to stay positive. For many years, our small delivery truck sported a bug shield with these words on it, a gift to me from MaryEllen.

Chaptalize: The process of adding sugar to fruit juices before fermentation with the goal of raising the finished alcohol content.

Coliform: A very common bacteria found nearly everywhere and, when found in a water well, will likely require a UV treatment system to be installed.

Crump: Legal term used by our country lawyer to mean "die."

EBITDA: Accounting term I learned while day trading: Earnings Before Interest, Taxes, Depreciation, and Amortization.

Eichenhofer: Surname of my friend Hank, a farm worker and former boss at IBM.

French Drains: Shallow man-made trenches filled with stone and covered with earth, created in farm fields to drain excess surface water.

Fk:** The usual utterance when things go wrong on the farm.

Geosmin: The smell of soil and rain.

Herpetology: The study of reptiles. The word is noted here only because in my early youth, when I was turtle farming, I was unaware of what to call my activity.

Imbibition: To take on liquid as in the first stage of a seed's germination.

Instar: Growth stages in immature insects.

Inversion: Farm speak used on a cold morning to label when there is a layer of warm air sitting on a layer of freezing air over one's orchard.

Lenticel: Tiny pores on the surface of an apple which allow it to breathe.

Lignification: The process of turning into wood.

Maceration: A process, used primarily in making red wine that involves steeping grape skins and solids in wine after fermentation, when alcohol acts as a solvent to extract color and tannins.

Marmorated Stink Bug: Fairly new fruit pest imported from China. Has the appearance of what could have been a WWI tank design or perhaps an alien creature in a 1950s sci-fi movie.

Mastitis: A common bacterial infection affecting cow, sheep, and goat udders.

Milorganite: Dried and pelletized human waste used as a fertilizer and deer repellent; very stinky.

Murphy's Law: Fictional farm law in effect at all times, loosely translated from an ancient Gaelic guru, meaning "If it can go wrong, it will go wrong."

Mycelium: The vegetative part of a fungus and essential for most plants' existence.

Next year: A phrase too often muttered—in farming and in sports—during a bad year.

Phenology: The study of cyclic and seasonal natural phenomena, especially in relation to plant and animal life, and one of my favorite words.

Photosynthesis: The process by which green plants transform light energy into chemical energy.

Physics: The study of energy, matter, and their interactions. I often speak of this field of science because most of its principles are employed on our farm over the course of a growing season.

Potassium metabisulfite, KMBS: An antioxidant and anti-microbial agent used in drug production and the food industry. We used it as needed as a wine stabilizer.

Pretty Woman: My favorite song, sung by Roy Orbison and released in 1964.

Profit: An imaginary condition seldom found on a farm.

Regulations: Rules that governments continuously produce to stifle profit.

Reverse osmosis: A sugar concentrating process used in producing maple syrup, which reduces sap boiling time.

ROI: Return on investment.

Schist: A type of metamorphic rock.

Shrinkage: The loss of fruit volume in a bushel of apples over time in a cold storage cooler.

Sport: Not always basketball or tennis. In the plant world, from a biological perspective, a sport is a spontaneous mutation that produces offspring with abnormal variation from its parents.

Spotted Wing Drosophila: Pesky fruit fly imported from China.

Sublimation: The process of a solid changing to a gas without passing through a liquid state. An example would be snow evaporating into the air on a cold day without becoming water first. One of the few words I stumped my wife with.

Supersedure: The natural replacement of an existing queen bee by a new queen in the same hive.

Sweetbread: An organ called thymus found in cows, reluctantly cooked by my first wife.

Tertiary: The third and weakest bud in a grapevine, which we hope survives an exceptionally cold winter that kills the primary and secondary buds.

Testamentary: Legal term used by our country lawyer to do with clarity and intent of one's official will.

Transpiration: The process of water movement through a plant and its evaporation from aerial parts.

Twenty-four-seven: Represents the hours and days farm life can ask of you.

Tupping: A term used in Scotland describing the mating process of rams and ewe sheep. Has nothing to do with our farm, but I thought you might like to add a new word to your vocabulary.

Veraison: Signals the onset of ripening in the life cycle of a grapevine. Red grapes begin to transition from green to red at this stage.

Wifetime: A marriage interval.

Yes!: A word I have come to use as I age when I achieve any minor success; stated loudly, with force and enthusiasm, accompanied by a thrusted airborne fist.

Zurk: Common name for a grease fitting on farm equipment.

Noteworthy Sayings

"Unknown outpaces known, like to do outpaces done."
—Kristin Kimball, *The Dirty Life*

"The fields are a clock read in colors."
—Kristin Kimball, *The Dirty Life*

"Eat food, not too much, mostly plants."
—Michael Pollan, *In Defense of Food*

"We realize the infinite is in the finite of each instant."
—Unknown Zen Master

"If it wasn't for next year, we wouldn't have a good year."
—A phrase often expressed by farmers

"There are only two ways to live your life. One is as though nothing is a miracle. The other is as though everything is a miracle." —Albert Einstein

"Blessed is the man who plants a tree under whose shade he knows he will never sit."
—Conveyed to me by Andy Watson, a farmer and friend

"Some people dream of success while others wake up and work hard at it." —Napoleon Hill

"Whoever mentions money first is the loser."
        —Frank Hoeffner, a farmer and friend

"Weather, often described as "normal," is an imaginary condition derived from extremes."   —Doug Glorie

'Life is like a snowball. All you need is wet snow and a really long hill."   —Warren Buffet

"Without farmers, you would be hungry, naked, and sober."
 —Jessica Whitaker Allen, Ted Talks contributor, farmer

"It might not seem like it at the time, but in my experience, I've found things usually work out for the best."
      —Daniel S. Dempsey, Sr., my father-in-law

"Expect the worst but hope for the best."
—A philosophy that I have practiced during my adult life.

Acknowledgements

I WAS INSPIRED TO WRITE THIS BOOK first BY MY WIFE, MaryEllen. I have been married to MaryEllen for thirty-one years, and together, we have endured, enjoyed, and laughed through hundreds of unique farm experiences. Along the way, she said, "We should write a book." Turns out that I was the one who wrote this book, and frankly, she was not entirely happy with my decision. However, her suggestions for story subjects and content enabled me to expand the breadth and scope of this book. MaryEllen had, when I met her, ten years of experience teaching English to Deaf students. She has a perfect command of the English language; I have never heard her mispronounce a word. She has read and edited each chapter no less than three times and has made countless corrections for spelling and grammar. It is unlikely you will discover any errors like dangling participles (which sound painful), except perhaps in those places where I overruled her suggested corrections. My book is a far superior product because of her dedicated effort!

Additional inspiration for writing this book came to me from my mother, Caroline. She had written several short books describing life in rural Orange County, New York, during the 1930s. I revisit these writings from time to time and am reminded of how simple life was ninety years ago. These recorded stories are priceless to me and my family.

I want to thank the George and Tillie Hoeffner family for hiring me during the mid-sixties to work on their farm, where I learned much and enjoyed countless new experiences that I treasure to this day. I want to thank their son Frank, who became my mentor and a second brother to me.

I want to thank my beta readers Frank Hoeffner, John Morabito, Richard Mangone, Joel Truncali, Dan Heavens, Ralph Winfield, and Jan Kahn for their valuable comments.

Thanks to the Quimby family, especially Howard, who had their fifty-four-acre inheritance on the market at the right time, so I could buy my dream farm and experience forty-one years of creative agriculture.

My children, Doug and Michele, may have liked me to spend more time with them during the eighties, as I worked on our farm before my IBM job in the morning and after work in the afternoon into evening, and on weekends and holidays, but to their credit and thanks also to their mother, Jo, still grew up to become creative, compassionate, ethical, successful people.

I was additionally motivated to record my thoughts and experiences after reading *Epitaph for a Peach* by David Masumoto, *Letter to a Young Farmer* by Gene Logsdon, and *The Dirty Life* by Kristin Kimball.

About the Author

Doug's agricultural journey began at the age of seven at the fringe of the Village of Montgomery, NY, and continues today at the age of seventy-six in Ulster County, NY. He is a graduate of Orange County Community College and Penn State University with a degree in Mechanical Engineering. He was employed by IBM, Poughkeepsie, NY, for twenty-three years. His time was divided between his responsibilities at IBM and various agricultural endeavors, eventually purchasing a fifty-four-acre farm, which became Glorie Farms and Glorie Farm Winery, and which was sold in 2020.

Doug is a member of the New York Farm Bureau, Cornell Cooperative Extension of Eastern New York, a member and a director of Cornell Hudson Valley Research Lab, past president and member of Mid-Valley Growers Coop, and co-founder and president of Hudson Valley Cabernet Franc Coalition.

He resides on a thirty-six-acre retirement farm near the top of the Marlboro Mountains with his wife, MaryEllen, where they grow wine grapes, plums, apples, Christmas trees, garlic, and pumpkins.

www.ingramcontent.com/pod-product-compliance
Lightning Source LLC
Chambersburg PA
CBHW071511160426
43196CB00010B/1485